1998

$2.00

2-3-19

D0467242

By Roger von Oech

A Whack on the Side of the Head

A Kick in the Seat of the Pants

Roger von Oech's Creative Whack Pack

Roger von Oech's Ancient Whacks of Heraclitus

A Whack on the Side of the Head

How You Can Be More Creative

Roger Von Oech

MJF BOOKS
NEW YORK

Published by MJF Books
Fine Communications
Two Lincoln Square
60 West 66th Street
New York, NY 10023

A Whack on the Side of the Head
LC Control Number 01-130250
ISBN 1-56731-457-0

Published by arrangement with Warner Books.

Book design by Roger von Oech
Text illustrations by George Willett

Manufactured in the United States of America on acid-free paper

MJF Books and the MJF colophon are trademarks of Fine Creative Media,
Inc.

10   9   8   7   6   5   4   3   2   1

To Wendy, Athena, and Alex

Table of Contents

6. That's Not My Area 101

7. Don't Be Foolish 113

8. Avoid Ambiguity 137

9. To Err Is Wrong 155

10. I'm Not Creative 165

A Whack on the Other Side of the Head 171

Ancient Whacks of Heraclitus 195

Preface

Welcome to *A Whack on the Side of the Head.* It's about the ten mental locks that prevent you from being more creative — and what you can do to open them. I hope you enjoy reading it.

Many of the ideas presented here come from my experiences working as a creative thinking consultant. Over the past two decades, I've had an opportunity to work with many creative people in a variety of industries and disciplines. This book contains stories, anecdotes, insights and ideas that came out of these workshops, as well as my own thoughts about what you can do to be more creative.

Indeed, I believe that this book contains the fundamentals of creative thinking. Whether you're a junior in high school, an account executive at an advertising agency, a software programmer, or a mother raising a family, I think that you'll find some useful ideas in these pages.

I'd like to thank the following people who have made a difference in this book: Wiley Caldwell, Bob Metcalfe, Jack Grimes, Nansey Neiman, Bill Shinker, Larry Kirshbaum, Anthony Qaiyum, Amy Einhorn, Mel Parker, Nancy Parker, Bob Wieder, Lance Shaw, Dan Zadra, Tim Hurson, Franca Leeson, and Doug King.

Many thanks to George Willett for his illustrations.

Most of all, I'd like to thank my family — especially my wife Wendy — for their ideas and encouragement.

Good luck, and Happy Whacking!

Roger von Oech
Atherton, California
February 16, 1998

A Whack on the Side of the Head

Mental Sex

Exercise: In my seminars, I like to start the participants off with the following exercise. Take a moment to do it.

1. When was the last time you came up with a creative idea?

☐ This morning
☐ Yesterday
☐ Last week
☐ Last month
☐ Last year

2. What was it?

3. What motivates you to be creative?

The answers I get usually run something like this: "I found a way to debug a software program"; "I thought up a new fund-raising strategy for our school"; "I discovered a way to sell a new application to a hard-to-satisfy client"; "I developed a new geometry curriculum"; "I motivated my daughter to do her homework"; or, "I decorated the living room around a different color."

Not long ago, I met a man who told me that he got his last creative idea a year ago. "This must have been *some* idea to have overshadowed everything else this year," I thought to myself, and asked him what it was. "I found a quicker way home from work," he replied.

I guess this person wasn't very motivated. He seemed to be saying, "Everything is fine," and there's no reason to deviate

from what's worked in the past. But he made me think: why be creative? Why challenge the rules? Why run the risk of failing and looking foolish?

I can think of two good reasons. The first is change. When things change and new information comes into existence, it's no longer possible to solve current problems with yesterday's solutions. Over and over again, people are finding out that what worked two years ago won't work today. This gives them a choice. They can either bemoan the fact that things aren't as easy as they used to be, or they can use their creative abilities to find new answers, new solutions, and new ideas.

A second reason for generating ideas is that it's a lot of fun. Indeed, I like to think of creative thinking as the "sex of our mental lives." Ideas, like organisms, have a life cycle. They are born, they develop, they reach maturity, and they die. So we need a way to generate new ideas. Creative thinking is that means, and like its biological counterpart, it's also pleasurable.

What Is Creative Thinking?

Exercise: Let's suppose that you're a marketing hot shot. You get a call from the president of a large company and learn that somehow his inventory system has fouled up, and his company now has a $1,000,000 over-supply of ball bearings. Your task is to think of things to do with the ball bearings, using them either one-at-a-time or in combinations. Take a minute to list your ideas.

I once asked advertising legend Carl Ally what makes the creative person tick. Ally responded, "The creative person wants to be a know-it-all. He wants to know about all kinds of things: ancient history, nineteenth century mathematics, current manufacturing techniques, flower arranging, and hog futures. He never knows when these ideas might come together to form a new idea. It may happen six minutes later or six years down the road. But the creative person has faith that it will happen."

I agree. Knowledge is the stuff from which new ideas are made. Nonetheless, knowledge alone won't make a person creative. I think that we've all known people who knew lots of facts and nothing creative happened. Their knowledge just sat in their crania because they didn't think about what they knew in any new ways. The real key to being creative lies in what you do with your knowledge.

Creative thinking requires an outlook that allows you to search for ideas and play with your knowledge and experience. With this outlook, you try different approaches, first one, then another, often not getting anywhere. You use crazy, foolish and impractical ideas as stepping stones to practical new ideas. You break the rules occasionally, and explore for ideas in unusual outside places. And, in the end, your creative outlook enables you to come up with new ideas.

Speaking of a creative outlook, how did you do with the ball bearing exercise? What ideas did you generate? Here are some possibilities:

 Use them as level testers.

 Sew them into a canvas vest and use them as "weight clothing" for athletes-in-training.

 Make furniture out of them — like bean bag chairs — to be used in public places. Since they'd be heavy, they wouldn't get stolen.

 Make jewelry out of them: earrings, bracelets, and necklaces.

 Use them as confetti at a punk rock concert.

Serve them as robot caviar (when your "home robot" is having friends over).

Put them on the bottom of uneven curtains and use them as curtain weights.

The point of this exercise is that an idea, concept, or thing — in this case a ball bearing — takes its meaning from the context in which you put it. If you change its context, it will take on a different meaning. For example, transferring a ball bearing from the "things that reduce friction" context to that of "shiny and pretty things" gives us all kinds of jewelry and art ideas. Emphasizing its "mass" characteristics allows us to think of "weight" ideas, such as curtain weights. Thus, changing contexts is one way to discover the possibilities of your resources. Here are some examples of people who used this type of thinking to create new ideas.

The first is Johann Gutenberg. What Gutenberg did was to combine two previously unconnected ideas: the wine press and the coin punch. The purpose of the coin punch was to leave an image on a small area such as a gold coin. The function of the wine press was, and still is, to apply force over a large area to squeeze the juice out of grapes. One day, Gutenberg, perhaps after he'd drunk a goblet of wine, asked himself, "What if I took a bunch of these coin punches and put them under the force of the wine press so that they left their image on paper?" The resulting combination was the printing press and movable type.

Navy Commander Grace Hopper had the task of explaining the meaning of a "nanosecond" to some non-technical computer users. (A nanosecond is a billionth of a second, and it's the basic time interval of a supercomputer's internal clock.) She wondered:

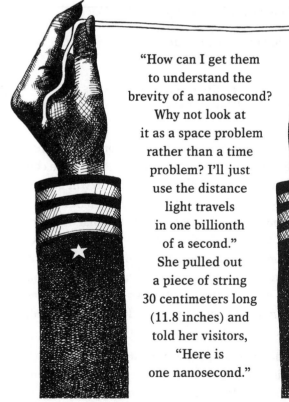

"How can I get them
to understand the
brevity of a nanosecond?
Why not look at
it as a space problem
rather than a time
problem? I'll just
use the distance
light travels
in one billionth
of a second."
She pulled out
a piece of string
30 centimeters long
(11.8 inches) and
told her visitors,
"Here is
one nanosecond."

In the second century B.C., a young Greek librarian had the job of trying to think of a more efficient way to order and retrieve the thousands of manuscripts that he had stored away. "How should I order these?" he wondered. "By subject? By author? By color?" Then he thought of the alphabet. His contemporaries thought of it simply as a series of phonetic symbols — *alpha, beta, gamma, delta, epsilon* — that create words when joined together. This librarian decided to de-emphasize the alphabet's linguistic qualities and emphasize the letters' order in relation to one another. He put all the documents beginning with *gamma* after those beginning with *beta* but in front of those beginning with *delta*. In the process, he created alphabetization, the primary means for ordering, storing, and retrieving information.

In 1792, the musicians of Franz Joseph Haydn's orchestra were mad because the Duke had promised them a vacation, but continually had postponed it. They asked Haydn to talk to the Duke about getting some time off. Haydn thought for a bit, decided to let music do the talking, and wrote the "Farewell Symphony." The performance began with a full orchestra, but as the piece goes along, it is scored to need fewer and fewer instruments. As each musician finished his part, he blew out his candle and left the stage. They did this, one by one, until the stage was empty. The Duke got the message and gave them a vacation.

One day Pablo Picasso went outside his house and found an old bicycle. He looked at it for a little bit and took off the seat and the handle bars. Then he welded them together to create the head of a bull.

And then there's my daughter Athena. On her third birthday, I gave her a small box with sixteen colored cubes in it. She picked it up, shook it, and told me that it was a rattle. She opened it up and said that it was a wallet and the cubes were money. Then she piled the cubes up, and they became a birthday cake.

Each of these examples illustrates the creative mind's power to transform one thing into another. By changing perspective and playing with our knowledge, we can make the ordinary extraordinary. In this way, wine presses squeeze out information, string is transformed into nanoseconds, labor grievances become symphonies, and bicycle seats turn into bulls' heads. The Nobel prize winning physician Albert Szent-Györgyi put it well when he said:

Discovery consists of looking at the same thing as everyone else and thinking something different.

Here are four quick exercises to give you a chance to "think something different."

Exercise: An eccentric old king wants to give his throne to one of his two sons. He decides that a horse race will be run and the son who owns the slower horse will become king. The sons, each fearing that the other will cheat by having his horse run less fast than it is capable, ask the court fool for his advice. With only two words the fool tells them how to make sure that the race will be fair. What are the two words?

Exercise: Can you think of a way in which you put a sheet of newspaper on the floor so that when two people stand face to face on it, they won't be able to touch one another? Cutting or tearing the paper is not allowed. Neither is tying up the people or preventing them from moving.

Exercise: What is this figure?

Exercise: Shown below is the Roman numeral seven. By adding only a single line, turn it into an eight.

VII

This is pretty easy; all you have to do is add a vertical line to the right of the VII to create an eight: VIII. Want something a little more challenging? Shown below is a Roman numeral nine. By adding only a single line, turn it into a 6.

IX

Some people put a horizontal line through the center, turn it upside down, and then cover the bottom. This gives you a Roman numeral VI. But if you're "thinking something different," you might put an "S" in front of the IX to create "SIX." If you did this, you've taken the IX out of the context of Roman numerals and put it into the context of Arabic numerals spelled out in English. What prevents some people from doing this is that even with only three examples of Roman numerals — VII, VIII, and IX — they get locked into the context of Roman numerals. Let's look for another answer. Can you think of other ways in which you can add a single line to "IX" and turn it into a 6?

IX

Another solution might be to add the line "6" after IX. Then you get IX6, or one times six. Here the "X" no longer represents "10" or the English letter "X" but rather the multiplication sign. The point: everybody has a lot of knowledge; by shifting the contexts in which you think about it, you'll discover new ideas.

(Switch horses. Try putting the newspaper in a doorway — door closed — with the two people standing on each side. If you look at it one way, it's a bird. If you look at it another way, it could be a question mark. If you turn it upside down, it looks like a seal juggling a ball on its nose.)

Mental Locks

Why don't we "think something different" more often? There are several main reasons. The first is that we don't need to be creative for most of what we do. For example, we don't need to be creative when we're driving on the freeway, or riding in an elevator, or waiting in line at a grocery store. We are creatures of habit when it comes to the business of living — everything from doing paperwork to tying our shoes to haggling with telephone solicitors. For most of our activities, these routines are indispensable. Without them, our lives would be in chaos, and we wouldn't get much accomplished. If you got up this morning and started contemplating the bristles on your toothbrush or questioning the meaning of toast, you probably wouldn't make it to work. Staying on routine thought paths enables us to do the many things we need to do without having to think about them.

Another reason we're not more creative is that we haven't been taught to be. Much of our educational system is an elaborate game of "guess what the teacher is thinking." Many of us have been taught that the best ideas are in someone else's head.

There are times, however, when you need to be creative and generate new ways to accomplish your objectives. When this happens, your own belief systems may prevent you from doing so. Here we come to a third reason why we don't "think something different" more often. Most of us have certain attitudes that lock our thinking into the status quo and keep us thinking "more of the same." These attitudes are necessary for most of what we do, but they get in the way when we're trying to be creative.

I call these attitudes **"mental locks."** There are ten mental locks in particular that I've found to be especially hazardous to our thinking. They are listed on the next page. As you can well imagine, it's difficult to get your creative juices flowing if you're always being practical, following the rules, afraid to make mistakes, or under the influence of any other mental lock.

1. The Right Answer.

2. That's Not Logical.

3. Follow the Rules.

4. Be Practical.

5. Play Is Frivolous.

6. That's Not My Area.

7. Don't Be Foolish.

8. Avoid Ambiguity.

9. To Err Is Wrong.

10. I'm Not Creative.

Opening Mental Locks

So, how do we open these mental locks? Let's turn to the following story for a possible answer.

A creativity teacher invited one of his students over to his house for afternoon tea. They talked for a bit, and then came time for tea. The teacher poured some into the student's cup. Even after the cup was full, he continued to pour. The cup overflowed and tea spilled out onto the floor.

Finally, the student said: "Master, you must stop pouring; the tea is overflowing — it's not going into the cup."

The teacher replied, "That's very observant. The same is true with you. If you are to receive any of my teachings, you must first empty out what you have in your mental cup."

Moral: We need the ability to unlearn what we know.

From our examples, we can see that Gutenberg forgot that wine presses only squeeze grapes — the "right answer"; Hopper didn't realize that everyday package-string was "outside the area" of supercomputing; Haydn didn't understand that equating music and labor grievances was a "foolish" idea; and Picasso broke the "rule" that bicycle seats are for sitting on.

Without the ability to temporarily forget what we know, our minds remain cluttered with ready-made answers, and we never have an opportunity to ask the questions that lead off the beaten path in new directions. Since the attitudes that create mental locks have all been learned, one key to opening them is to temporarily unlearn them — to empty our mental cup.

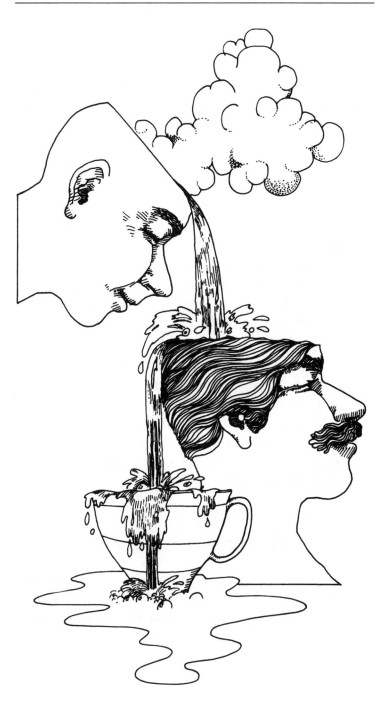

This sounds like a simple technique, but sometimes it's difficult to apply. Often we have integrated these mental locks so well into our thinking and behavior that we are no longer aware that we're being guided by them. They have become habits. The danger of habits is that a person can become a prisoner of familiarity. The more often you do something in the same way — whether it's cooking a meal or managing a project — the more difficult it is to do it in any other way. You get stuck in how you already think about things.

So, sometimes we need a little help to open the mental locks. Let's return to our creativity teacher once more.

> At another lesson the teacher and the student are discussing a problem. Despite lengthy conversation, the student doesn't seem to understand the point the teacher is making.
>
> Finally, the teacher picks up a stick and gives him a whack on the side of the head with it. Suddenly, the student begins to grasp the situation and "think something different."
>
> **Moral:** Sometimes, nothing short of "a whack on the side of the head" can dislodge the assumptions that keep us thinking "more of the same."

Getting Whacked

Like the student, we all need an occasional "whack on the side of the head" to shake us out of routine patterns, to force us to re-think our problems, and to stimulate us to ask the questions that may lead to other right answers.

"Whacks" come in all shapes, sizes, and colors. They have

one thing in common, however. They force you — at least for the moment — "to think something different." Sometimes you'll get whacked by a problem or a failure. Sometimes it'll be the result of a joke or a paradox. And sometimes it will be a surprise or an unexpected situation that whacks you. Here are some examples:

◆ It could result from your getting fired from a job, or failing to obtain a performance raise.

◆ It could happen when a teacher tells you that she thinks that you have a special talent in an area you'd never thought much about and assigns a project — due next Friday — to help you develop it.

◆ It might happen when the supplier for a vital sub-component of your best selling product unexpectedly goes on strike and you're forced to scramble to find a new source. When the dust has cleared you discover that the new vendor is far superior in product quality.

◆ It could come when you recognize a relationship between two things you thought were unconnected such as a spiral galaxy and a spinning ice skater.

◆ It could happen when you observe the second hand of your watch in a mirror. (Try it!)

◆ It could be the result of traveling to another country, say England, and being forced to drive on the left side of the road.

◆ It could happen when someone tells you that the answer to your problem is the sixth word down on page 247 of your dictionary, and when you look it up, you discover that she's right.

◆ It could happen when you break your leg and you realize how much you took your ambulatory habits for granted.

◆ It could be a question you never thought about:

◈ "What's the rationale behind many cars having two keys — one for the door and the other for the ignition?"

◈ "Is the push-button telephone the death of the word 'dialing'?"

◈ "If one synchronized swimmer drowns, do the others have to drown too?"

◈ "If camels are the 'ships of the desert' why aren't tugboats the 'camels of the sea'?"

◈ "Is it against the law to yell 'Movie!' in a crowded fire house?"

◈ "If there were fewer sponges would the ocean be deeper?"

◈ "If you put an orchid in your refrigerator and a day later it starts smelling like salami, does the salami start smelling like an orchid?"

◈ "Which way is clockwise on a digital watch?"

◈ "Do sportscasters in India yell, 'Holy Cow'?"

◈ "If we call oranges 'oranges,' why don't we call bananas 'yellows,' or apples 'reds'?"

◆ It could be a joke:

Q: What is the difference between a cat and a comma?

A: A cat has its claws at the end of its paws and a comma is the pause at the end of a clause.

Those ideas or situations that cause you to get off your routine paths and "think something different" are whacks to your thinking.

Sometimes getting a whack on the side of the head can be the best thing to happen to you. It might help you spot a potential problem before it arises. It could help you discover an opportunity that wasn't previously apparent. Or, it could help you generate some new ideas.

Thomas Edison serves as a good example for the benefits of getting whacked. As a young man, his primary interest was improving the telegraph. He invented the multiplex telegraph, the ticker tape machine (a variation of the telegraph), and other telegraphic innovations. Then, in the early 1870's, the financier Jay Gould bought out the Western Union telegraph system thereby establishing a monopoly over the industry. Edison realized that as long as Gould owned the system, the need to be innovative was reduced. This whacked him out of his telegraphic routine, and forced him to look for other ways in which to use his talent. Within a few years, he came up with the light bulb, the power plant, the phonograph, the film projector, and many other inventions. He may have discovered these anyway, but Gould's whack was certainly a stimulant in getting him to look for other opportunities.

A more recent example is Rex McPherson — a third-generation citrus grower in central Florida. In the early 1980's, he lost 85% of his citrus stock due to severe freezes two consecutive years. This loss forced him to re-think his whole citrus-growing concept. Rex realized that the trees (planted by his grandfather in the 1930's and 1940's) had been placed fairly far apart because land at that time was cheap. Land values have sky-rocketed since then, and he realized that if he wanted to stay in the citrus business he had better re-think his concept. He decided to use new hybrids and irrigation techniques in order to plant the trees close together. As a result, not only has his yield increased significantly, but also the closeness of the trees has helped to inhibit freezing. The whack (the loss due to the freezes) was painful at the time, but it provided Rex with the impetus to "think something different."

Here's a personal whack. Several years ago, the pool where my Masters swimming team works out was closed for a month of maintenance. During the downtime, the members had to prac-tice with other clubs in the area. When we were reunited a month later, there was a great outpouring of new workout ideas. One person had been with a team that had low rest-interval work-outs. Another came back with a heartbeat interval workout. Another found a new type of ankle pull-buoy. All these ideas were discovered because we were forced to break our routine.

And here's a final personal whack that I can't resist shar-ing. On my son's 7th birthday, our family went out to dinner. Alex ordered salmon. When our dinners arrived, he looked at his plate. Next to the salmon lay a wedge of lemon. "What's this for?" he asked. I explained that it was used to season the fish. "But you'd better taste it first," I warned. A moment later, I heard him exclaim, "Yow! That's the sourest lemon I've ever tasted." Of course, I meant for him to taste the fish first to see how much lemon juice to put on it. Who's to say what the right answer is? I've never looked at condiments in the same way since. Maybe we should taste more lemons to jolt our thinking.

Summary

We don't need to be creative for most of what we do, but when there is a need to "think something different," our own attitudes can get in the way. I call these attitudes **mental locks**.

Mental locks can be opened in one of two ways. The first technique is to become aware of them, and then to temporarily forget them when you are trying to generate new ideas. If that doesn't work, maybe you need a "whack on the side of the head." That should dislodge the presuppositions that hold the locks in place.

For the remainder of the book, we'll examine each of the mental locks and find out what kinds of ideas can be generated by temporarily opening them. We'll also take a look at some techniques to whack our thinking. Along the way we'll meet some interesting head-whackers: artists, poets, revolutionaries, magicians, explorers, fools, and self-trusting innovators.

Let's Get Rolling!

1. The Right Answer

Exercise: Five figures are shown below. Select the one that is different from all the others.

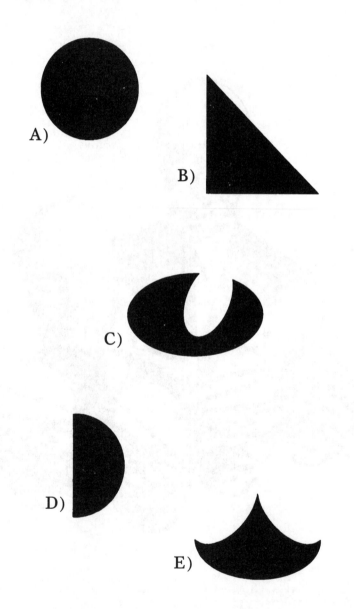

Learning How to Think

Children enter school as question marks and come out as periods.

— Neil Postman, Educator

Life can be like a big noisy party with people talking, music playing, and glasses clinking. But even with all of this noise, it's possible for you to understand the person across from you. Or the one thirty feet away. That's because our attention is selective — we can tune in certain things and tune out others.

See for yourself. Take a look around where you're sitting and find four things that have "red" in them. Go ahead and do it. With a "red" mindset, you'll find that red jumps right out at you: a red telephone book, red in the blister on your index finger, red in the wallpaper, and so on. Similarly, whenever you learn a new word, you hear it eight times in the next three days. In like fashion, you've probably noticed that after you get a new car, you see that make everywhere. That's because people find what they are looking for. If you look for beauty, you'll find beauty. If you look for conspiracies, you'll find conspiracies. It's all a matter of setting your mental channel.

Where do you learn how to set your mental channel? One important source is your formal education. There you learn what is appropriate and what is not. You learn many of the questions you use to probe your surroundings. You learn where to search for information, which ideas to pay attention to, and how to think about these ideas. Your educational training gives you many of the concepts you use to order and understand the world.

Speaking of education, how did you do on the five-figure exercise on the previous page? If you chose figure B, congratulations! You've picked the right answer. Figure B is the only one that has all straight lines. Give yourself a pat on the back!

Some of you, however, may have chosen figure C, thinking that C is unique because it's the only one that is asymmetrical. And you are also right! C is the right answer. A case can also be made for figure A: it's the only one with no points. Therefore, A is the right answer. What about D? It is the only one that has both a straight line and a curved line. So, D is the right answer too. And E? Among other things, E is the only one that looks like a projection of a non-Euclidean triangle into Euclidean space. It is also the right answer. In other words, they are all right depending on your point of view.

But you won't find this exercise in school. Much of our educational system is geared toward teaching people to find "the right answer." By the time the average person finishes college, he or she will have taken over 2,600 tests, quizzes, and exams — many similar to the one you just took. The "right answer" approach becomes deeply ingrained in our thinking. This may be fine for some mathematical problems where there is in fact only one right answer. The difficulty is that most of life isn't this way. Life is ambiguous; there are many right answers — all depending on what you are looking for. But if you think there is only one right answer, then you'll stop looking as soon as you find one.

When I was a sophomore in high school, my English teacher put a small chalk dot like the one below on the blackboard.

She asked the class what it was. A few seconds passed and then someone said, "A chalk dot on the blackboard." The rest of the class seemed relieved that the obvious had been stated, and no one else had anything more to say. "I'm surprised at you," the teacher told the class. "I did the same exercise yesterday

with a group of kindergartners, and they thought of fifty different things it could be: an owl's eye, a cigar butt, the top of a
telephone pole, a star, a pebble, a squashed bug, a rotten egg,
and so on. They had their imaginations in high gear."

In the ten year period between kindergarten and high school,
not only had we learned how to find the right answer, we had
also lost the ability to look for more than one right answer. We
had learned how to be specific, but we had lost much of our
imaginative power.

An elementary school teacher told me the following story
about a colleague who had given her first graders a coloring
assignment:

> The instructions said: "On this sheet of paper, you
> will find an outline of a house, trees, flowers, clouds,
> and sky. Please color each with the appropriate colors."

One of the students, Patty, put a lot of work into her drawing. When she got it back, she was surprised to find a big black "X" on it. She asked the teacher for an explanation. "I gave you an 'X' because you didn't follow the instructions. Grass is green not gray. The sky should be blue, not yellow as you have drawn it. Why didn't you use the normal colors, Patty?"

Patty answered, "Because that's how it looks to me when I get up early to watch the sunrise."

The teacher had assumed that there was only one right answer. The practice of looking for the "one right answer" can have serious consequences in the way we think about and deal with problems. Most people don't like problems, and when they encounter them, they usually react by taking the first way out they can find — even if they solve the wrong problem. I can't overstate the danger in this. If you have only one idea, you have only one course of action open to you, and this is quite risky in a world where flexibility is a requirement for survival.

An idea is like a musical note. In the same way that a musical note can only be understood in relation to other notes (either as a part of a melody or a chord), an idea is best understood in the context of other ideas. If you have only one idea, you don't have anything to compare it to. You don't know its strengths and weaknesses. I believe that the French philosopher Emilé Chartier hit the nail squarely on the head when he said:

Nothing is more dangerous than an idea when it is the only one we have.

For more effective thinking, we need different points of view. Otherwise, we'll get stuck looking at the same things and miss seeing things outside our focus.

The Second Right Answer

A leading business school did a study that showed that its graduates performed well at first, but in ten years, they were overtaken by a more streetwise, pragmatic group. The reason according to the professor who ran the study: "We taught them how to solve problems, not recognize opportunities. When opportunity knocked, they put out their 'Do Not Disturb' signs."

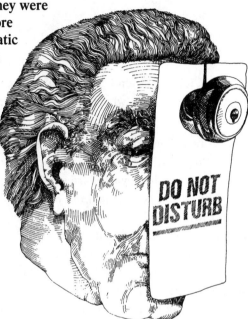

Not long ago I did a series of creative thinking workshops for the executive staff of a large computer company. The president had called me in because he was concerned about the stagnant thinking environment at the top. It seemed that whenever his subordinates would make a proposal, that's all they'd make — just one. They wouldn't offer any alternative ideas. Since they had been trained to look for the right answer, they usually didn't go beyond the first one they found. The president knew that it was easier to make good decisions if he had a variety of ideas from which to choose. He was also concerned with how conservative this "one-idea" tendency had made his people's thinking. If a person were presenting only one idea, he would generally propose the "sure thing" rather than take a chance on a less likely off-beat idea. This state of affairs created a less than ideal climate for generating innovative ideas. I told them that one way to be more creative is to:

Look for the second right answer.

Often, it is the second right answer which, although off-beat or unusual, is exactly what you need to solve a problem in an innovative way.

One technique for finding the second right answer is to change the questions you use to probe a problem. For example, how many times have you heard someone say, "What is the answer?" or "What is the meaning of this?" or "What is the result?" These people are looking for *the* answer, and *the* meaning, and *the* result. And that's all they'll find — just one. If you train yourself to ask questions that solicit plural answers like "What are the answers?" or "What are the meanings?" or "What are the results?" you will find that people will think a little more deeply and offer more than one idea. As the Nobel Prize winning chemist Linus Pauling put it:

The best way to get a good idea is to get a lot of ideas.

You may not be able to use all of them, but out of the number you generate you may find a few that are worthwhile. This is why professional photographers take so many pictures when shooting an important subject. They may take twenty, sixty or a hundred shots. They'll change the exposure, the lighting, the filters, and so on. That's because they know that out of all the pictures they take, there may be only a few that capture what they're looking for. It's the same thing with creative thinking: you need to generate a lot of ideas to get some good ones.

Inventor Ray Dolby (the man who took "hiss" out of recorded music) has a similar philosophy. He says:

> Inventing is a skill that some people have and some people don't. But you can learn how to invent. You have to have the will not to jump at the first solution, because the really elegant solution might be right around the corner. An inventor is someone who says, "Yes, that's one way to do it, but it doesn't seem to be an optimum solution." Then he keeps on thinking.

When you look for more than one right answer, you allow your imagination to open up. How do you keep a fish from smelling? Cook it as soon as you catch it. Freeze it. Wrap it in paper. Leave it in the water. Switch to chicken. Keep a cat around. Burn incense. Cut its nose off.

One technique for finding more answers is to change the wording in your questions. If an architect looks at an opening between two rooms and thinks, "What type of *door* should I use to connect these rooms?" that's what she'll design — a door. But if she thinks "What sort of *passageway* should I put here?" she may design something different like a "hallway," an "air curtain," a "tunnel," or perhaps a "courtyard." Different words bring in different assumptions and lead your thinking in different directions.

Here's an example of how such a strategy can work. Several centuries ago, a curious but deadly plague appeared in a small village in Lithuania. What was curious about this disease was its grip on its victim; as soon as a person contracted it, he'd go into a deep almost deathlike coma. Most died within a day, but occasionally a hardy soul would make it back to the full bloom of health. The problem was that since eighteenth century medical technology wasn't very advanced, the unafflicted had quite a difficult time telling whether a victim was dead or alive.

Then one day it was discovered that someone had been buried alive. This alarmed the townspeople, so they called a town meeting to decide what should be done to prevent such a situation from happening again. After much discussion, most people agreed on the following solution. They decided to put food and water in every casket next to the body. They would even put an air hole from the casket up to the earth's surface. These procedures would be expensive, but they would be more than worthwhile if they would save people's lives.

Another group came up with a second, less expensive, right answer. They proposed implanting a twelve inch long stake in every coffin lid directly above where the victim's heart would be. Then whatever doubts there were about whether the person was dead or alive would be eliminated as soon the coffin lid was closed. What differentiated the two solutions were the questions used to find them. Whereas the first group asked, "What should we do if we bury somebody *alive?*" the second group wondered, "How can we make sure everyone we bury is *dead?*"

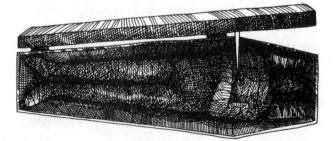

I'd like to conclude this "right answer" chapter with one of my favorite Sufi stories.

Two men had an argument. To settle the matter, they went to a Sufi judge for arbitration. The plaintiff made his case. He was very eloquent and persuasive in his reasoning. When he finished, the judge nodded in approval and said, "That's right, that's right."

On hearing this, the defendant jumped up and said, "Wait a second, judge, you haven't even heard my side of the case yet." So the judge told the defendant to state his case. He, too, was very persuasive and eloquent. When he finished, the judge said, "That's right, that's right."

When the clerk of court heard this, he jumped up and said, "Judge, they both can't be right." The judge looked at the clerk and said, "That's right, that's right."

Moral: Truth is all around you; what matters is where you place your focus.

That's
Right!

That's
Right!

Summary

Much of our educational system has taught us to look for the one right answer. This approach is fine for some situations, but many of us have a tendency to stop looking for alternative right answers after the first right answer has been found. This is unfortunate because often it's the second, or third, or tenth right answer which is what we need to solve a problem in an innovative way.

There are many ways to find the second right answer — asking "what if," playing the fool, reversing the problem, breaking the rules, etc. Indeed, that's what much of this book is about. The important thing, however, is to look for the second right answer, because unless you do, you won't find it.

TIP: The answers you get depend on the questions you ask. Play with your wording to get different answers. One technique is to solicit plural answers. Another is to ask questions that whack people's thinking. One woman told me that she had a manager who would keep her mind on its toes by asking questions such as: "What are three things you feel totally neutral about?" and "Which parts of your problem do you associate with tax returns and which parts with poetry?"

2. That's Not Logical

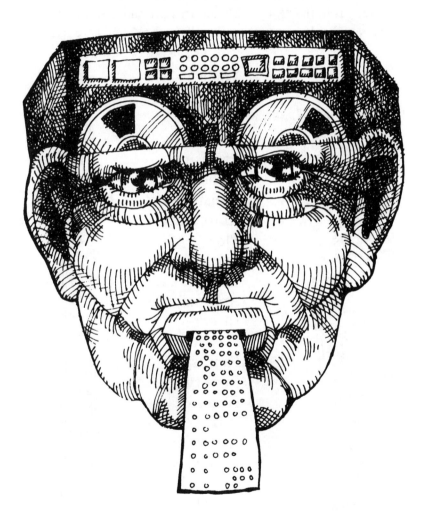

Exercise: Take a blank sheet of paper and draw a vertical line down the center. On the top left, write the word "Soft," and on the top right write the word "Hard." Now take a moment and look at the following concepts. Those you associate with being soft, put in the "Soft" column. Those you associate with being hard, put in the "Hard" column. This is a subjective exercise, but you should have a general feeling for soft and hard things.

Logic
Metaphor
Dream
Reason
Precision
Humor
Consistency
Ambiguity
Play
Work
Exact
Approximate
Direct
Focused
Fantasy
Reality
Paradox
Diffuse
Analysis
Hunch
Generalization
Specifics
Child
Adult

Now take a moment to think about this question: how would you compare the "Hard" list with the "Soft" one? Objective versus subjective? Quantitative versus qualitative? Masculine versus feminine?

Soft and Hard Thinking

At this point, you might be wondering about the purpose of this exercise. Well, the difference between soft and hard helped solve a problem for me. Not long ago, I stayed up late one night and tried to think of all the different types of thinking there are. Here's a partial list:

Logical thinking	Mythical thinking
Conceptual thinking	Poetic thinking
Analytical thinking	Non-verbal thinking
Primitive thinking	Analogical thinking
Critical thinking	Lyrical thinking
Foolish thinking	Practical thinking
Convergent thinking	Divergent thinking
Weird thinking	Ambiguous thinking
Reflective thinking	Constructive thinking
Visual thinking	Thinking about thinking
Symbolic thinking	Surreal thinking
Digital thinking	Concrete thinking
Metaphorical thinking	Fantasy thinking

I must have thought of close to a hundred different types of thinking. Then I asked myself, "How can I order them? What patterns do they have in common?" I thought about these questions for some time, but came up empty.

I was about to go to bed when I remembered the words of Kenneth Boulding. Boulding was an economist by profession, but more than that, he was a student of life. What he said was this:

There are two kinds of people in this world: those who divide everything into two groups, and those who don't.

At that moment I was feeling like a member of the former group. I thought: "Why not apply this binary insight to the different types of thinking and divide them into two groups." But what would the differentiating factors be? I thought of opposites: good/bad, strong/weak, inside/outside, big/small, masculine/feminine, living/dying, and so on, but none of these expressed what I was looking for. And then it hit me: why not Soft and Hard?

If you are like a lot of people, your "Soft" and "Hard" lists probably looked something like this:

Soft	**Hard**
Metaphor	Logic
Dream	Reason
Humor	Precision
Ambiguity	Consistency
Play	Work
Approximate	Exact
Fantasy	Reality
Paradox	Direct
Diffuse	Focused
Hunch	Analysis
Generalization	Specific
Child	Adult

As you can see, things on the hard side have a definite right and wrong answer; on the soft side, there may be many right answers. On the hard side, things are black and white; on the soft side there are many shades of gray (to say nothing of orange, purple, and magenta!). A few of you might say that you can pick up the things on the hard side — like a bar of metal.

The soft things are a little more difficult to grab onto — like a handful of water.

Soft thinking has many of the characteristics on the "Soft" list: it is metaphorical, approximate, humorous, playful, and capable of dealing with contradiction. Hard thinking, on the other hand, tends to be more logical, precise, exact, specific, and consistent. We might say that hard thinking is like a spotlight. It is bright, clear, and intense, but the focus is narrow. Soft thinking is like a floodlight. It is more diffuse, not as intense, but covers a wider area.

Soft thinking tries to find similarities and connections among things, while hard thinking focuses on their differences. For example, a soft thinker might say that a cat and refrigerator have a lot in common, and then proceed to point out their similarities (they both have a place to put fish, they both have tails, they both come in a variety of colors, they both purr, they both have a lifetime of about fifteen years, etc.). The hard thinker would establish the cat and the refrigerator as being part of two different sets.

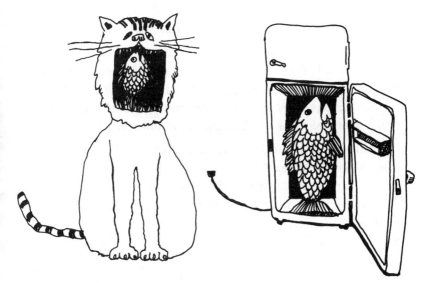

A person using soft thinking might ask a question such as, "What would furniture look like if our knees bent the other way?" The hard thinker would say, "What materials should be used in manufacturing to optimize the rate of return on this new line of chairs?"

The Creative Process

Where do you use soft and hard thinking? To answer this question, we should turn to the creative process. There are two main phases in the development of new ideas: an **"imaginative"** phase and a **"practical"** one.

In the imaginative phase, you generate and play with ideas. In the practical phase, you evaluate and execute them. To use a biological metaphor, the imaginative phase sprouts the new ideas and the practical phase cultivates and harvests them.

In the imaginative phase, you ask questions such as: What if? Why not? What rules can we break? What assumptions can we drop? How about if we looked at this backwards? Can we borrow a metaphor from another discipline? The motto of the imaginative phase is: **"Thinking something different."**

In the practical phase, you ask questions such as: Is this idea any good? Do we have the resources to implement it? Is the timing right? Who can help us? What's the deadline? What are the consequences of not reaching the objective? The motto of the practical phase is: **"Getting something done."**

Both types of thinking play an important role in the creative process, but usually during different phases. Soft thinking is effective in the imaginative phase when you are searching for new ideas, and manipulating problems. Hard thinking, on the other hand, is best used in the practical phase when you are evaluating ideas, narrowing in on practical solutions, running risk-analyses, and preparing to carry the idea into action.

A good analogy for the need for both types of thinking in the creative process is a potter making a vase. If you've ever done any work with clay, you know that it's a lot easier to shape, mold, and throw the clay if it has some softness to it (brittle clay is hard to shape). By the same token, after the vase has been shaped, it has no practical value until it has been put into a kiln and fired. Both the soft and the hard elements are required but at different times.

If soft and hard thinking have their strengths, they also have their weaknesses. Thus, it is important to know when each is *not* appropriate. Soft thinking in the practical phase can prevent the execution of an idea; here firmness and directness are preferable to ambiguity and dreams. Conversely, hard thinking in the imaginative phase can limit the creative process. Logic and analysis are important tools, but an overreliance on them — especially early in the creative process — can prematurely narrow your thinking.

That's Not Logical

The first and supreme principle of traditional logic is the law of noncontradiction. Logic can comprehend only those things that have a consistent and non-contradictory nature. This is fine except that most of life is ambiguous: inconsistency and contradiction are the hallmarks of human existence. As a result, the number of things that can be thought about in a logical manner is small, and an overemphasis on the logical method can inhibit your thinking.

Some people, however, have little use for soft thinking. Their feeling toward it is "that's not logical." When faced with a problem, they immediately bring in their hard thinking strategies. They say, "Let's get down to brass tacks." They never give themselves an opportunity to consider steel tacks, copper tacks, plastic tacks, sailing tacks, income tax, syntax, or contacts. If you use a little soft thinking early in the creative process, you may still end up going with the "brass tacks," but at least you will have considered alternatives.

Our educational system does a fairly good job of developing hard thinking skills, but there is not much to develop soft thinking. As a matter of fact, much of our education is geared toward eliminating soft thinking, or at best, teaching us to regard it as an inferior tool. Human intelligence is a complicated phenomenon, and yet many of our formal notions of intelligence are based on logic and analysis. Musical ability, decorating, painting, and cooking seem to have no place in many test makers' conceptions of intelligence. As creativity educator Edward de Bono points out, "If someone says he has learned to think, most of us assume that he means he has learned to think logically."

There is another reason for the "that's not logical" mental lock. As an historian of ideas, I've noticed that the models people use to understand mental processes reflect the technology of their time. For example, in the 17th century, people thought about the mind as though it were a mirror or a lens, and this "reflects" the advances made then in the fields of optics and lens making. The Freudian model of mind, developed in the late 19th and early 20th centuries, seems based on the ubiquity of the steam engine locomotive. Ideas billow up from the subconscious to the conscious in the same way steam moves from boiler to compression chamber. In the early twentieth century, the mind was viewed by some as a vast telephone switching network with circuits and relays running through the brain.

For the past thirty years, we've had a new model of mind: the computer. This model does a good job of describing certain aspects of our thinking. For example, we have "input" and "output" and "information processing." There is also "feedback," "programming," and "storage."

This is fine as far as it goes, but some people take this model literally and think that the mind really *is* a computer. Indeed, they may not only dismiss the soft types of thinking for not being "logical," but even treat other people like machines.

I believe that the mind is not only a computer that processes information, it's also a museum that stores experiences, a device that encodes holograms, a playground in which to play, a muscle to be strengthened, a workshop in which to construct thoughts, a debating opponent to be won over, a cat to be stroked, a funhouse to be explored, a compost pile to be turned, and forty-three others. There are a lot of right ways to model the mind all depending on what you think is important.

One of the saddest consequences of the "that's not logical" mental lock is that its prisoner may not pay attention to one of the mind's softest and most valuable creations: the intuitive hunch. Your mind is constantly recording, connecting, and storing unrelated knowledge, experiences, and feelings. Later, it combines this disparate information into answers — hunches — to the problems you're facing, if you simply ask, trust, and listen. These hunches, for no apparent logical reason, might lead you to trying a different problem-solving approach, going out on a blind date, betting on the underdog in a sporting event, taking a spontaneous vacation, or ignoring a trusted friend's advice.

Exercise: What hunches have you had recently? Which ones did you listen to? How did things work out? What decision are you currently facing? What does your gut tell you to do?

Making the Strange Familiar

To combat the dangers of creative rigor mortis due to excessive hard thinking, I would like to introduce one of my favorite soft thinking tools. I'll introduce it with an exercise. As you do this exercise, think of yourself as a poet. This is a high compliment: our word poet comes from the classical Greek word *poietes* which meant not only "poet" but also "creator."

Exercise: What do the following have in common?

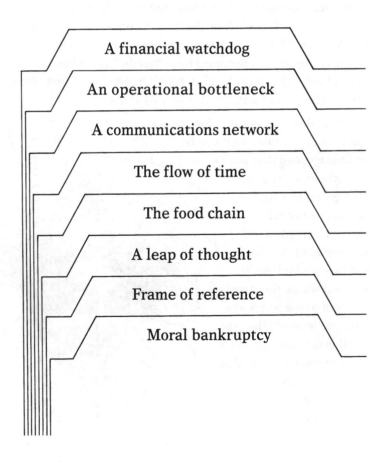

A financial watchdog

An operational bottleneck

A communications network

The flow of time

The food chain

A leap of thought

Frame of reference

Moral bankruptcy

In addition to everything else, they are all metaphors. They all connect two very different universes of meaning through some similarity they share. In doing so, metaphors help us to understand one idea by means of another. For example, we understand the nature of a particular financial function by comparing it to a watchdog (they both protect), the passing of time to a river (flow), and the feeding interrelationship of the animal world to a chain (links).

The key to metaphorical thinking is similarity. In fact, this is how our thinking grows: we understand the unfamiliar by means of the similarities it has with what is familiar to us. For example, what were the first automobiles called? That's right, "horseless carriages." And the first locomotives were called "iron horses." We refer to resemblances between things all of the time. We say that hammers have "heads," tables have "legs," roads have "shoulders," cities have "hearts," and beds have "feet." It's all very soft, but it *is* how we think.

How about a metaphor for metaphors? Let's suppose that you fly to Chicago, and that you've never been there before. You get off the airplane and rent a car. What's the first thing you do? Get a map of the city to see how it's laid out, to find out where the streets are, and to see where the sites are located. The map itself is not Chicago, but it does give you a basic idea of the structure of the city. So, a metaphor is a mental map.

Metaphors are quite useful in helping you get a different slant on a problem. For example, in the 17th century William Harvey looked at the heart not as a muscle or an organ, but as a "pump." This led to his discovery of the circulation of blood. In the early twentieth century, Danish physicist Niels Bohr developed a new model of the atom by comparing it to the solar system. Within this framework, he figured that the sun represented the nucleus and the planets represented the electrons.

Another example: several years ago I had a client whose sales were flat even though there was a boom in the marketplace for the products they offered. We decided to make a metaphor for their company. We decided that their company was like a full service restaurant. Its menu (product line) was large, but there were many restrictions on what could be purchased — for example, a customer could not order chili with veal. Since the individual chefs (division managers) decided what was on the menu, there was no consistency in their offerings. This led to their having specialized waiters (salespeople). A typical result? A customer couldn't buy pasta from a steak waiter or hot dogs from a fish waiter. We developed this metaphor further, but it quickly became clear to us that the large, restricted product line confused their customers, and was the main source of their flat sales.

Metaphors are also effective in making complex ideas easier to understand. Some years ago, I had to memorize the various parts of a computer operating system. I didn't want to memorize all the details but I did need to know the various relationships of the parts to one another. So I said to myself, "Why don't I make a metaphor? This operating system is like an automobile. This part is like the chassis, this part is like the engine, this part is like the steering wheel, and so on." Whenever I needed to remember the operating system, I just brought to mind my metaphorical picture of the automobile.

Exercise: Make a metaphor for a problem you're currently dealing with or a concept you're developing. To do it, simply compare your concept to something else and then see what similarities you can find between the two ideas. Basically, you're using one idea to highlight another. See how far you can extend the comparison.

I've found that some of the most fertile (and easiest to develop) metaphors are those in which there is some action taking place. You might try comparing your concept to several of these:

Running for political office
Disciplining a ten year old
Cooking a fancy meal
Fighting the government
Starting a revolution
Negotiating a contract
Going fishing
Putting out a fire
Fighting a disease
Doing standup comedy
Conducting an orchestra
Making a sales call
Courting a mate

Going on a diet
Performing a magic trick
Colonizing a territory
Building a house
Spreading propaganda
Prospecting for gold
Planting a garden
Having a baby
Arranging flowers
Impersonating the 17th c.
French mathematician
Rene Descartes and then
Disappearing

Exercise: The Bible is quite metaphorical. Whether it's Jesus talking in parables or the prophets using similes to foretell the future, you'll find many ideas expressed metaphorically. This is particularly true in the *Book of Proverbs.* Here is a quiz from *Proverbs.* Connect the metaphor on the left side with the idea it represents on the right side.

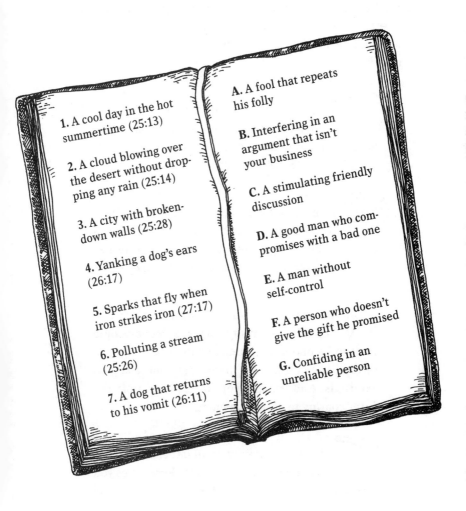

1. A cool day in the hot summertime (25:13)

2. A cloud blowing over the desert without dropping any rain (25:14)

3. A city with broken-down walls (25:28)

4. Yanking a dog's ears (26:17)

5. Sparks that fly when iron strikes iron (27:17)

6. Polluting a stream (25:26)

7. A dog that returns to his vomit (26:11)

A. A fool that repeats his folly

B. Interfering in an argument that isn't your business

C. A stimulating friendly discussion

D. A good man who compromises with a bad one

E. A man without self-control

F. A person who doesn't give the gift he promised

G. Confiding in an unreliable person

The Meaning of Life

As you may have guessed by now, metaphors are one of my passions, and so I hope you'll excuse me for one more metaphorical indulgence.

One question I have is, "What is the meaning of life?" To find the answer, I have asked my seminar participants to make a metaphor for life. Their ideas can be put into two groups: those that deal with food, and those that don't. Here is the meaning of life:

Life is like a bagel. It's delicious when it's fresh and warm, but often it's just hard. The hole in the middle is its great mystery, and yet it wouldn't be a bagel without it.

Life is like eating grapefruit. First you have to break through the skin; then it takes a couple of bites to get used to the taste, and just as you begin to enjoy it, it squirts you in the eye.

Life is like a banana. You start out green and get soft and mushy with age. Some people want to be one of the bunch while others want to be top banana. You have to take care not to slip on externals. And, finally, you have to strip off the outer coating to get at the meat.

Life is like cooking. It all depends on what you add and how you mix it. Sometimes you follow the recipe and at other times, you're creative.

Life is like a jigsaw puzzle, but you don't have the picture on the front of the box to know what it's supposed to look like. Sometimes, you're not even sure if you have all the pieces.

 Life is like a maze in which you try to avoid the exit.

Life is like riding an elevator. It has lots of ups and downs and someone is always pushing your buttons. Sometimes you get the shaft, but what really bothers you are the jerks.

 Life is like a poker game. You deal or are dealt to. It includes skill and luck. You bet, check, bluff, and raise. You learn from those you play with. Sometimes, you win with a pair or lose with a full house. But whatever happens, it's best to keep on shuffling along.

 Life is like a puppy dog always searching for a street full of fire hydrants.

Life is like a room full of open doors that close as you get older.

What do you think life is like?

Summary

Logic is an important creative thinking tool. Its use is especially appropriate in the practical phase of the creative process when you are evaluating ideas and preparing them for action. When you're searching for and playing with ideas, however, excessive logical thinking can short-circuit your creative process. That's because the imaginative phase is governed by a different logic that is best described as metaphorical, fantastic, elliptical, and ambiguous.

For more and better ideas, I prescribe a good dose of soft thinking in the imaginative phase of the creative process, and a hearty helping of hard thinking in the practical phase.

TIP: The metaphor is an excellent tool to help you "think something different." Think of yourself as a poet, and look for similarities around you. If you have a problem, make a metaphor. This should give you a fresh slant on it.

TIP: Go on "metaphor hunts." Pay attention to the metaphors people use to describe what they are doing. For example, have you ever noticed how meteorologists use the "War Model of Weather" to describe their science?

TIP: Pay attention to the metaphors you use in your own thinking. As glorious a tool as metaphors are, they can easily imprison your thinking if you're not aware how much they're guiding your thoughts.

TIP: Remember, it's an illogical world. The glow worm isn't a worm. A firefly isn't a fly. The English horn isn't English (French) or a horn (woodwind). The Harlem Globetrotters didn't play a game in Harlem until they'd been playing for forty years. We name or refer to things not be precise, but to grasp a sense of them.

3. Follow the Rules

Patterns: The Rules of the Game

Order is heav'n's first law.

— Alexander Pope, Poet

Let's suppose that you're watching television in your living room with some friends. Someone walks into the room, and as he does, he trips over a chair and knocks it down. This person picks up the chair and excuses himself for the commotion he's caused. What's your impression of this person? You probably think he's a klutz, right?

Okay, ten minutes later, another person walks into the room, and she too falls over the chair. Twenty minutes later, another person walks into the room, and the whole scene is repeated again. What's your opinion now? Probably that the chair is in the wrong place. Congratulations, you have recognized a pattern! You might even generalize this pattern into a rule such that anybody walking into the room will trip over the chair unless, of course, it's moved.

Suppose I gave you the following series of numbers:

1, 4, 9, 16, 25, 36, 49

More than likely, you would quickly recognize a pattern, namely that each of the numbers is the square of its position in the series. You might feel so confident that you would predict the next numbers in the series to be 64 and 81. Again, you have made a rule based on a pattern you have recognized. What if you saw this list:

Painted Eggs
Fireworks
Candy Canes
John Philip Sousa music
Shamrocks
Jack-o'-Lanterns

At first, you probably wouldn't recognize much similarity between painted eggs and fireworks, but after reading through the rest of the list, you would realize that these things are all associated with American holidays. If we continued the list, you wouldn't be surprised to find egg nog, heart candy, the Unknown Soldier, and cherry trees.

With these three examples, we recognize another pattern, namely, that the human mind is very good at recognizing patterns. Indeed, I think that much of what we call "intelligence" is our ability to recognize patterns. We recognize sequences (buds turn into flowers), cycles (plankton yields conform to a strict four year boom-and-bust cycle), shapes (cracks in dried mud usually form 120° angles), similarities (stellar galaxies and water emptying out of a bath tub spiral in the same way), and probabilities (the likelihood of throwing a "seven" at a crap table).

People see patterns everywhere — even when none is intended. A good example is the night sky. In Fig. 1, we see a portion of the spring sky in the northern hemisphere.

Figure 1) A Portion of the Spring Sky

Looks like a bunch of stars, right? Well, thousands of years ago, the ancients looked up, emphasized some of the stars, made a few connections, and came up with the figure of a lion — a celestial Rorschach!

Figure 2) The Constellation Leo

Patterns give us the power to understand the world, and as a consequence, they *rule* our thinking — they become the rules according to which we play the game of life.

Challenging the Rules

If constructing patterns were all that were necessary for creating new ideas, we'd all be creative geniuses. There is, however, another element involved in the creative process. The following exercise highlights this element. Take a moment to do it.

Exercise: Shown below is a maze. Starting at point A, work your way through the maze to point B. Use a pen or pencil to keep track of your progress.

That wasn't too difficult. Now take a look at what you you've done. To solve this problem, you probably used one of the following three strategies. The first is: you started at A and worked your way through to B. Whenever you came to a dead end, you backtracked out of it and then moved forward anew. So, backtracking is an effective strategy in this problem.

A second approach is to start at B and then move backwards to A. We use this method for much of what we do. If you have a project that must be finished three months from today, you might think to yourself: "Where should I be in two months? Where should I be next month? Where should I be next week?" So, working backwards is another effective strategy.

A third solution is to break the rules. How about drawing a straight line from A to B? Maybe going all the way around the border? How about tearing the page out of the book and then folding it in half so that B touches A? Some people object that breaking the rules goes against the directions. That may be true but sometimes you have to do that in order to be innovative. As artist Pablo Picasso put it:

Every act of creation is first of all an act of destruction.

Thus, creative thinking is not only constructive, it's also destructive. As we stated in the opening chapter, creative thinking involves playing with what you know, and this may mean breaking out of one pattern in order to create a new one. An effective creative thinking strategy is to play the revolutionary and challenge the rules. Here are some examples.

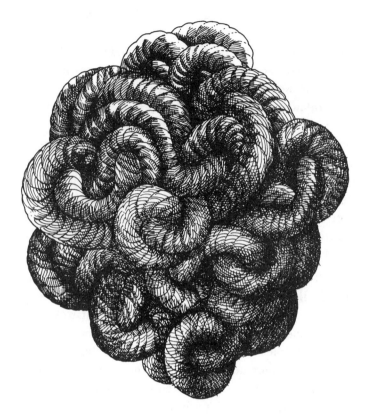

In the winter of 333 B.C., the Macedonian general Alexander and his army arrive in the Asian city of Gordium to take up winter quarters. While there, Alexander hears about the legend surrounding the town's famous knot, the "Gordian Knot." A prophecy states that whoever is able to untie this strangely complicated knot will become king of Asia. This story intrigues Alexander, and he asks to be taken to the knot so that he can attempt to untie it. He studies it for a bit, but after fruitless attempts to find the rope ends, he is stymied. "How can I unfasten the knot?" he asks himself. He gets an idea: "I'll make up my own knot-untying rules." He pulls out his sword and slices the knot in half. Asia is fated to him.

With his postulation that the earth circles the sun, the Polish astronomer Copernicus broke the rule that the universe is anthropocentric. With her evocative love odes, the Greek poet Sappho broke the rule that great lyric poetry was outside the province of women. With his use of trailing codas and double orchestral fugues, Beethoven broke the rules on how a symphony should be composed. With his lightning attacks of mechanized equipment the German general Ernst Rommel broke the rules on how to fight a battle. With his equating mass and energy as different forms of the same phenomenon, Einstein broke the rules of Newtonian physics. Think about it: almost every advance in art, medicine, agriculture, engineering, marketing, politics, education, and design has occurred when someone challenged the rules and tried another approach.

Such rule-breaking happens in sports as well. Take swimming. Until the 1920's, there were only three competitive swimming strokes — freestyle, backstroke, and breaststroke — and each had specific rules that described how it was to be performed. The rules of breaststroke stated that both arms must be pulled together underwater and then recovered simultaneously back to the start of the pulling position to begin the next stroke. Most people interpreted this arm recovery to mean an *underwater* recovery. In the 1920's, however, someone challenged the rules and reinterpreted this arm recovery to be an *out-of-the-water* recovery. Since this new "breaststroke" was about 15% faster, people using the orthodox version couldn't effectively compete. Something had to be done. Finally, this new stroke — now known as the "butterfly" — won recognition as the fourth swimming stroke, and became an Olympic event in 1956. This has happened in other sports too. If the rules hadn't been changed along the way, there would still be jump balls after every field goal in basketball; foul balls wouldn't count as strikes in baseball; and football wouldn't have a passing game.

I have a friend I go to whenever I have a really tough problem to solve. After I explain it to him, invariably his first question is, "What rules can we break?" He knows that I have assimilated so many rules into my thinking that after a while they become blind assumptions. It's difficult to be innovative if you're following blind assumptions.

The creative thinker is constantly challenging the rules. Most people will say, "As a rule, if operation 'XYZ' is done in a certain way, it will get these results 'alpha-beta-gamma.'" Here, "XYZ" can be a marketing strategy, a way to teach drawing to third graders, a choreography system, an engineering process, a fund-raising technique, or a way to stuff a turkey. The creative thinker will play with "XYZ" and look for results *outside* the usual rules and guidelines. One organization I know has gone so far as to incorporate this philosophy into their motto:

Every rule here can be challenged except this one.

They feel that if they are following the same rules five years from now, they won't have advanced the state of their art. They know that the rule that worked last year is probably valid this year, but they won't know for sure unless they challenge it.

Follow the Rules

If you don't ask, "why this?" often enough, somebody will ask, "why you?"

— Tom Hirshfield, Physicist

Playing the revolutionary is easier said than done. One company president told me that his most difficult task is getting his subordinates to challenge the rules. He raises a good point. Why do people treat most problems and situations as closed ones with set rules, rather than as open ones that can be played with?

One main reason is that there is a lot of pressure in our culture to "follow the rules." This value is one of the first things we learn as children. We are told such things as: "No orange elephants," and "Don't color outside the lines." Our educational system encourages further rule-following. Students are usually better rewarded for regurgitating information than for playing with ideas and thinking originally. As a consequence, people feel more comfortable following the rules than challenging them.

From a practical standpoint, this value makes sense. In order to survive in society, you have to follow all kinds of rules. Shouting in a library, crying out "fire" in a packed theater, or cheating on your income taxes are three things *not* to do. If, however, you're trying to generate new ideas, then the value "follow the rules" can be a mental lock because it means: "Think about things only as they are."

WARNING: When I encourage you to challenge the rules, I'm not advocating you to do anything that's illegal, immoral, or unethical. Most of the rules you follow, however, aren't written down in some manual or book of legal statutes. In other words, they're unwritten rules such as the way you go to work, who cuts your hair, the typestyle you use most often, how your business forms are designed, what you say to people in elevators, or where you buy groceries. Unless you challenge them, you won't be more creative.

The Aslan Phenomenon

Creative Thinking may simply mean the realization that there is no particular virtue in doing things the way they have always been done.
— Rudolph Flesch, Educator

Challenging the rules is a good creative thinking strategy, but that's not all. Never challenging the rules brings with it at least two potential dangers. The first is you can get locked into one approach, method, or strategy without seeing that other approaches might be more appropriate. As a result, you may tailor your problems to the preconceptions that enable you to solve them that way.

A second reason that the rules should be challenged is the "Aslan Phenomenon." It runs as follows:

1. We make rules based on reasons that make a lot of sense.

2. We follow these rules.

3. Time passes, and things change.

4. The original reasons for the generation of these rules may no longer exist, but because the rules are still in place, we continue to follow them.

For example, I like to run, and I have five or six routes that I'll take depending on how far I want to go. One of these is a route that goes through my neighborhood for about four miles. As a rule, the run ends about two blocks from our house, because several years ago, when I started this route, there was a big, friendly golden retriever living at the house where I stopped.

His name was Aslan. After my run, I would take time to pet him, cool down, and steal his tennis ball. So stopping at Aslan's house became the rule for having a nice ending to a fun run.

But things have changed. His owner moved away and took Aslan with her. Nevertheless, whenever I take this route, I still stop at the same place — even though Aslan no longer lives there. There are probably more pleasurable places to end my run, but because I'm following an obsolete rule, I haven't looked for them.

Here's another example of the Aslan phenomenon. Take a look at the following configuration of letters:

Q W E R T Y U I O P

Are you familiar with them? You have undoubtedly seen this pattern many times. It is the top row of letters on a standardly configured typewriter or computer keyboard. It is known as the QWERTY configuration, and it has a fascinating history.

Back in the 1870's, Sholes & Co., a leading manufacturer of typewriters at the time, received many complaints from users about typewriter keys sticking together if the operator went too fast. In response, management asked its engineers to figure out a way to prevent this from happening. The engineers discussed the problem for a bit and then one of them said, "What if we slowed the operator down? If we did that, the keys wouldn't jam together nearly as much." The result was to have an inefficient keyboard configuration. For example, the letters "O" and "I" are the third and sixth most frequently used letters in the English language, and yet the engineers positioned them on the keyboard so that the relatively weaker fingers had to depress them. This "inefficient logic" pervaded the keyboard, and this brilliant idea solved the problem of keyboard jam-up.

Since that solution, the state of the art in typewriter and word-processing technology has advanced significantly. There are now typewriters and computers that can go much faster than any human operator can type. The problem is that the QWERTY configuration continues to be used even though there are faster configurations available. **Moral:** Once a rule gets in place, it's very difficult to eliminate even though the original reason for its generation has disappeared. Thus, creative thinking involves not only generating new ideas, but escaping from obsolete ones as well.

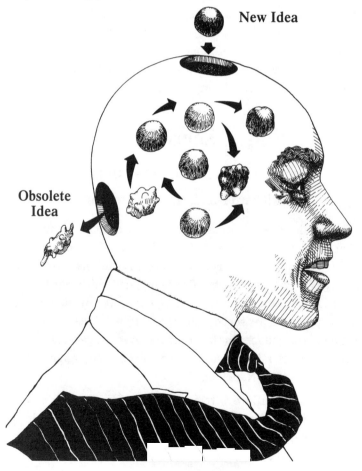

New Idea

Obsolete
Idea

Not long ago, I read about a group of Russian immigrants who have the tradition of celebrating New Year's Eve on the afternoon of December 30th. A reporter for the Los Angeles *Times* heard about this and, thinking that there was a story there, went out to interview them. "Why are you celebrating the new year thirty-six hours before everyone else?" she asked. One of them, a man in his late sixties, responded, "When we were growing up in the Soviet Union forty years ago, we were very poor, and we found that it was a lot cheaper to get a band on December 30th. That's how the tradition started." The curious thing is that most of these people are well off. They could easily afford lavish entertainment on New Year's Eve, and yet they still celebrate it on the previous afternoon. Almost every organization I've ever worked with — including my own — has some of this mentality of celebrating New Year's Eve early for an obsolete reason.

Slay A Sacred Cow

Sacred Cows make great steaks.

— Richard Nicolosi, Businessman

Some rules are so successful that they become immune to criticism. These are the "sacred cows." As a result, people are afraid to challenge them. For example, it is said that Frederick the Great (1712-1786) lost the Battle of Jena which was fought in 1806. This means that for twenty years after his death, the army perpetuated his successful organization instead of adapting to meet the changes in the art of war. Had his generals questioned Frederick's hallowed military tenets, they might have fared better against Napoleon.

Avoid falling in love with ideas. I got this advice from my printer. He said, "If you want to be successful, don't fall in love with a particular type style, because if you do, you'll want to use it everywhere — even in places where it's inappropriate." This

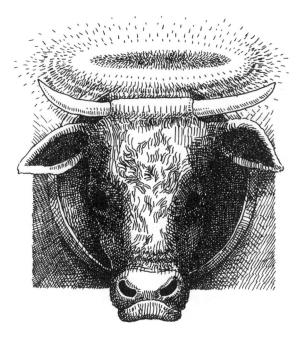

also applies to ideas. I've seen people fall in love with a certain approach, and then become unable to see the merits of alternative approaches. I think that one of life's great pleasures is falling out of love with a previously cherished idea. When that happens you're free to look for new ones.

Go after your sacred cows. Periodically inspect your ideas and beliefs to see if they are contributing to your thinking effectiveness. Ask yourself, "Why did this program, concept, project, or idea come to be?" Then follow this question with, "Do these reasons still exist?" If the answer is "no," then eliminate the idea. One person told me that he liked this link between elimination and innovation. He asked the eight people who worked with him to write down five things they didn't like about their jobs — ways of dealing with customers, paperwork, writing memos, policies, whatever. Curiously, all eight people had three similar things on their list. They focused on these, and were able to eliminate two of them as being obsolete.

Summary

Creative thinking is not only constructive, it's also destructive. Often, you have to break out of one pattern to discover another one.

Be flexible with the rules. Remember, breaking the rules won't necessarily lead to creative ideas, but it's one avenue. And staying on the same road may eventually lead to a dead end. After all, many rules outlive the purpose for which they were intended.

TIP: Play the revolutionary and challenge the rules — especially the ones you use to govern your day-to-day activities. If you usually start shaving on the left side of your face, tomorrow start on the right. If you never watch soap operas, watch some daytime television. If you usually listen to rock music, then listen to some jazz or classical music. If you usually work Monday through Friday, why not work the weekend and take the week off?

TIP: Have rule-inspecting and rule-discarding sessions. You may even find some motivational side benefits in this activity. Finding and eliminating outmoded rules can be a lot of fun. Perhaps Mark Twain had something like this in mind when he said, "One of life's most overvalued pleasures is sexual intercourse; and, one of life's least appreciated pleasures is defecation."

4. Be Practical

Exercise: Shown below is a design for a new chair. Write down three impressions you have about its value.

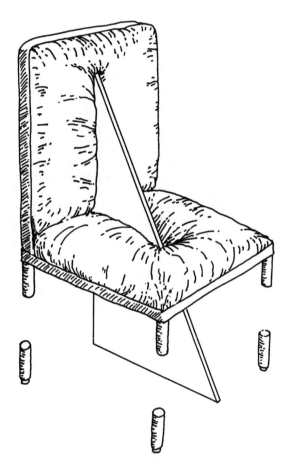

Design for a new chair

Our Imaginative Seedbed

Exercise: What would happen if gravity stopped for one second every day? What would things be like? What would land surfaces look like? How about oceans and rivers? How would life have developed under such conditions? Would living things have special "zero-gravity" adaptive features? How would buildings, houses, and furniture be designed? How about transportation systems? What about food?

Human beings occupy a special niche in the order of things. Because we have the ability to symbolize our experience, our thinking is not limited to the real and the present. This capability empowers our thinking in two major ways. First, it enables us to anticipate the future. We're able to ask ourselves: "Suppose it rains tomorrow. What would happen to our picnic? What alternative arrangements should be made?" By simulating such possibilities, we can plan for the future.

Second, since our thinking is not bound by real world constraints, we can generate ideas that have no correlate in the world of experience. You did this in the exercise about gravity.

Similarly, you do it whenever you dream or imagine anything that doesn't actually exist.

I call the realm of the possible our "imaginative seedbed." There are many good soft thinking tools for cultivating this seedbed. In this chapter, we'll focus on two of them: the "what if?" question and the "stepping stone."

Ask "What If?"

Asking "what if?" is an easy but powerful way to get your imagination going. There are two simple steps involved:

> **Step #1:** Simply ask "what if?" and then finish the question with some contrary-to-fact condition, idea, or situation.

> **Step #2:** Answer the "what if" question.

The "what if" question can be whatever you wish. The nice thing about "what-iffing" is that it allows you to suspend a few assumptions, and get into an imaginative frame of mind. Some examples:

◆ What if animals became more intelligent than human beings?

◆ What if men also had babies?

◆ What if pigs had wings?

◆ What if we elected our officials by lottery?

◆ What if people exuded a terrible smell from all their pores whenever they behaved unethically?

◆ What if human life expectancy were 200 years?

◆ What if all people carried their homes and property on their backs like turtles?

◆ What if the price of a barrel of fresh water and a barrel of petroleum were the same?

◆ What if we had to marry people who were at least twenty years older or younger in age?

◆ What if there were five sexes?

◆ What if when you looked in the mirror, there became two of you?

◆ What if people didn't need to sleep?

◆ What if trees developed the ability to move themselves up to 10 meters a day?

◆ What if people had to spend every third year outside the country where they were born?

Now, let's ask and answer one:

> ◆ What if we had seven fingers on each hand? Would we
> have two finger-opposing thumbs on each hand? If we
> did, would we have a better "grasp" on things? You could
> name your fingers after the days of the week, and if you
> didn't like something, you could flip that person a
> "Wednesday." If you were clumsy, you could say, "Sorry,
> I'm all weekends."

How would seven fingers on each hand affect sports?
How would we catch balls? Would we become more sure-
handed? Can't you just see some players, after a good
play, saying: "Gimme seven, gimme fourteen." That raises
an interesting point: maybe our number system would
be base 14 instead of base 10.

Would more people be in the jewelry business? What
kind of piano music would be written? What would hand
tools look like? How about typewriter and computer key-
boards. How would they be arranged? Would there be
more shift keys? Maybe instead of a keyboard there
would be "keyspheres" — balls with keys on them that
you squeezed to get the letters you wanted.

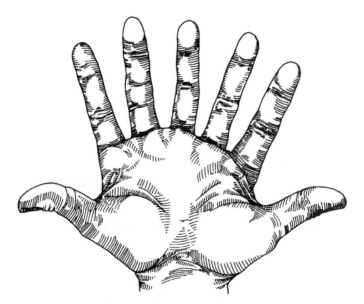

At the very least, this question makes us think about something we take very much for granted — our fingers.

You can see that asking "what if?" questions is not only a lot of fun, it also gives you the freedom to think along different lines. Who should whack himself with this soft thinking tool? Everybody — housewives, salespeople, children, teachers, comedians, coaches, politicians, doctors, florists, managers, and you — can benefit from asking "what if?" It's a way of freeing yourself from the deeply ingrained assumptions you have about your work and your personal life.

Here are two specific "what if" strategies for you to try.

Imagine How Others Would Do It

A good way to stretch your imagination is to ask "what if" someone else were solving your problem. How would this person — for example, Winston Churchill, Machiavelli, your mother, Leonardo da Vinci, Mother Teresa, the Three Stooges, Socrates, Jesus of Nazareth, Wonder Woman, the Godfather, a French chef, Sigmund Freud, Beethoven, Martin Luther King, or a seven year old girl — go about it? What assumptions would they bring in? What constraints would they ignore? What special twists would they give to it? What special expertise would they add? What innovative changes would they make?

For example, let's suppose that you're the principal of a high school. What if someone with a mindset like Walt Disney had your job? How would he approach it? What things would change? For one thing, there might be more emphasis on graphics and visual learning. Students would learn through experience, e.g., they might study the Civil War by making scenes of different battles. They would learn history by pretending they were the characters they were studying. Imagine the playground: students would learn physics and engineering from building rides for the school. The motto would be "If you don't take risks, you won't achieve what you want." Students would enjoy school more, thus boosting attendance. And there would be an emphasis on students learning creativity skills.

Whom do you respect for creative achievement? A leader in your field? A teacher? A parent? Now imagine that one of these is responsible for developing your concept. What would they do? How would they approach it?

Imagine You're the Idea

Another "what if?" technique is to imagine that you're the idea you're trying to develop. For example, suppose you're trying to improve the design of a toaster. What would it be like to actually be a toaster? How would you receive bread? What would it be like when your heating elements go on? What happens when seeds fall to the bottom? What's it like to cool down?

What if you are working to change the design of a parking meter? Now, imagine what it's like to be a parking meter. How does it feel when coins are inserted in you? What does it feel like when you have "expired"? How could you be easier to use? What would you look like if you took credit cards? How does the magnetic stripe feel? What sounds might you make?

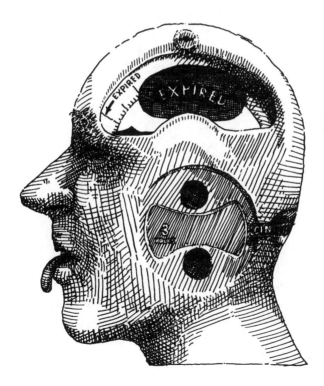

The results of such playful speculation can yield quite practical results. A noted scientist once asked himself, "What if I were an elevator falling through space at the speed of light? What if there was a hole in the side of the elevator? What if a shaft of light came through this hole into the elevator? What would happen? What would the light's behavior be?" By investigating the ramifications of such a possibility, Albert Einstein developed some of his early relativity concepts.

I have a friend I talk with about the creative process. She says she thinks that my ideas are interesting but that "what really happens in the inner chamber of creative thought is indistinguishable from magic." She makes a good point. Our thinking is quite magical. Try playing the magician — the one who specializes in asking the fantasy "what if" question.

The Stepping-Stone

"What if" questions, by themselves, may not produce practical, creative ideas. Thus, it may be necessary to use another thinking tool — the stepping-stone. Stepping-stones are simply provocative ideas that stimulate us to think about other ideas. Stepping-stones may be impractical or improbable, but their value consists not in how practical they are, but in where they lead your thinking. Remember, when you are in the imaginative phase of the creative process, real world constraints do not apply. It sometimes happens that an impractical idea leads to a practical, creative one. The following story is a good example of this phenomenon.

Several years ago, an engineer at a large chemical company asked the following question: "What if we put gunpowder in our house paint?" The people around him were somewhat taken aback, but the engineer continued.

Have you ever noticed what happens to paint after it's been on a house for five or six years? It chips and cracks and is very difficult to remove. There has to be a better way to get it off. If we put gunpowder in our house paint, we could blow it off the house.

The engineer had an interesting idea, but it had one drawback — it wasn't very practical. The people who were listening to this man, however, did something very much to their credit. They didn't evaluate his idea on the basis of its practical merits. On the contrary, they approached it as a stepping-stone which might lead them to a practical, creative solution. They thought, "What other ways are there to create a chemical reaction that would remove the old house paint?" This question opened up their thinking and eventually led to the idea of putting additives in their house paint. These additives would be inert until another solution containing other additives was applied to the old paint at a later date. At this point, a reaction would take place that would cause the paint to strip right off. That company went on to make such a process a reality.

Here's another example. A few years ago, a city in the Netherlands had a refuse problem. A once clean section of town had become an eyesore because people had stopped using the trash cans. There were cigarette butts, beer bottles, chocolate wrappers, newspapers, and other trash littering the streets.

Obviously, the sanitation department was concerned, so they sought ways to clean up the city. One idea was to double the littering fine from 25 guilders to 50 guilders for each offense. They tried this, but it had little effect. Another approach was to increase the number of litter agents who patrolled the area. This was more of the same, that is, another "punish the litterer" solution, and it, too, had little impact on the problem. Then somebody asked the following question:

> What if our trash cans paid people money when they put their trash in? We could put an electronic sensing device on each can as well as a coin-return mechanism. Whenever someone put trash in the can, it would pay him 10 guilders.

This idea, to say the least, whacked everyone's thinking. The what-iffer had changed the situation from a "punish the litterer" problem to a "reward the law abider" opportunity. The idea had one glaring fault, however; if the city implemented the idea, it would go bankrupt. Half of Europe would come to use their trash cans.

Fortunately, the people who were listening to this idea didn't evaluate it based on its practical merits. Instead, they used it as a stepping-stone and asked themselves: "What other ways are there in which we can reward people for putting their refuse in the trash cans?" This question led to the following solution. The sanitation department developed electronic trash cans which had a sensing unit on the top that would detect when a piece of refuse had been deposited. This would activate a tape recorder that would play a recording of a joke. In other words, joke-telling trash cans! Different trash cans told different kinds of jokes (some told bad puns while others told shaggy dog stories and still others told snappy one-liners) and soon developed reputations. The jokes were changed every two weeks. As a result, people went out of their way to put their trash in the trash cans, and the town became clean once again.

Here's a final example of the stepping-stone principle.

A group of researchers at a dog food company asked: What if we put nondigestible additives — for example, flower seeds — in our products? Dogs would then become delivery systems going about planting and fertilizing flowers in the neighborhood. Another additive might be a nontoxic fluorescent material. This would be especially appropriate in cities at night where pedestrians would know that the glowing object up ahead is something they don't want to step on.

This discussion didn't lead to any new dog food products, but it did lead to several practical cattle feed ideas. One is a way of putting grass seed in cattle feed as a way of reseeding range lands. Another is creating a fluorescent salt lick. Wild life rangers could then more closely monitor targeted animals. A third is a "pesticide" (nontoxic and nondigestible) that harmlessly passes through the cow to become part of the cow feces. Certain disease-breeding flies that are attracted to the feces are eliminated by their contact with it.

Be Practical

**The human mind likes a strange idea as
little as the body likes a strange protein
and resists it with a similar energy.**

— W.I. Beveridge, Scientist

Why don't people use "what if" thinking and stepping stones more often to generate ideas? There are three main reasons. The first is that when people look at new ideas, they tend to be critical and focus on what's out of whack. For example, what were your comments about the new chair design at the beginning of this chapter? If you're like a lot of people, you probably said something like:

▼ "It looks uncomfortable."

▼ "It's impractical. It would fall over
as soon as someone tried to sit on it."

▼ "It's ugly."

Notice that all of the comments are negative. Many people don't ask where the chair is going to be used or what the purpose is. What if it were to be used on the moon or underwater? Would that change your assessment?

In addition to finding out what's wrong with a new idea, it's important to focus in on what's worth building on. Sometimes a drawback can serve as a stepping stone to a practical, creative idea. For example:

▲ "Perhaps the blade is retractable; when
you want to keep your shedding dog or cat
off the chair, have the blade up. When you
want to sit down, retract it."

▲ "Meetings would be shorter and to the point."

▲ "It's a good chair for three o'clock in the afternoon when everyone's sleepy."

Here's an evaluation tip. When you judge new ideas, focus initially on their positive, interesting, and potentially useful features. This approach will not only counteract a natural negative bias, it will also enable you to develop more ideas. For example: what are five benefits to sleeping in your clothes?

A second reason that we don't ask "what if" more often is that this tool is low-probability in character. It's fairly unlikely that any particular "what if" question will produce a practical, creative idea. Thus, you may have to ask many "what if" questions and follow out many stepping stones before reaching a practical, creative idea. How many "what if" questions did Einstein ask himself before he boarded his imaginary elevator? A hundred? Two hundred? No matter. He eventuallÿ got a good idea which he probably wouldn't have gotten had he stayed in the practical realm. Thus, even though the likelihood of any given "what if" question reaching fruition is low, a few imaginative ideas will bear fruit in the world of action. Most people, however, don't feel they have the time to do this, so they limit themselves to the more practical "what is."

The third reason we don't use these tools is that we haven't been taught to. What happens to our imaginations as we mature? When we are young, they are cultivated in fairy tales and imagination games, but then we are told to "grow up." As people grow older, they get used to the "what is" of reality and forget about the possibilities that asking "what if" can generate. One of my workshop participants had this appraisal:

The amount a person uses her imagination is inversely proportional to the amount of punishment she will receive for using it.

Her implication: it's okay for children but not for adults to spend their time "what-iffing." We have been trained to respond to the unusual by saying, "That's not practical," instead of, "Hey, that's interesting; I wonder where that will lead our thinking." If the people who were discussing "gunpowder paint" or "coin-return trash cans" had said, "be practical," they never would have given themselves an opportunity to take an imaginative idea and turn it into a usable one. As Picasso put it:

Every child is an artist.
The problem is how to remain
an artist after growing up.

To be sure, you need to be practical for almost all of your daily activities. If you aren't, you probably won't survive very long. You can't live on imaginary food, or stop your car with "what if brakes" that save brake lining by working only 75% of the time. Being practical is important in the world of action, but practicality alone will not generate new ideas. The logic that works so well in judging and executing ideas may stifle the creative process if it prevents the artist in you from exploring unusual imaginative ideas.

Summary

This world was built by practical people who knew how to get into an imaginative frame of mind, listen to their imaginations, and build on the ideas they found there.

TIP: Each of you has an "artist" and a "judge" within you. The open-minded attitude of the artist typifies the kind of thinking you use in the imaginative phase when you're generating ideas. The evaluative outlook of the judge represents the kind of thinking you use in the practical phase when you're preparing ideas for execution. I recommend that you avoid bringing in your judge before your artist has had a chance to do her job. Premature evaluation can prevent conception.

TIP: Cultivate your imagination. Set aside time every day to ask yourself "what if" questions. Use the provocative answers you find as stepping-stones to new ideas. Although the likelihood that any given "what if" question will lead to a practical idea isn't high, the more often you practice this activity, the more productive you'll become.

TIP: The playwright Jerome Lawrence has an evaluation technique, the "creative no," that he uses whenever he's collaborating with someone else. It works like this: either member of the partnership can veto the other's ideas. However, when one partner does exercise this veto, he also takes responsibility for coming up with a new idea that both partners like. Thus, it's not only destructive, it's constructive as well.

5. Play Is Frivolous

Exercise: Here's a chance for you to use your imagination. What do the squares below look like to you? Try to think of at least four different things.

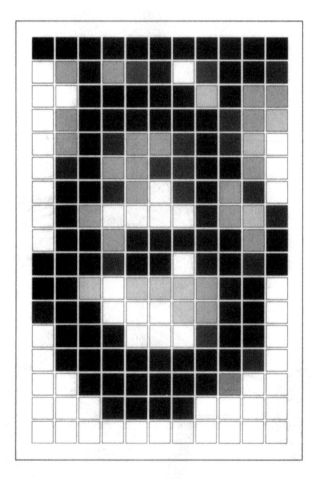

The Moment of Conception

What, then, is the right way of living? Life must be lived as play.

— Plato, Philosopher

Exercise: During what kinds of activities and situations do you get your ideas? For example, doing routine work, as a response to questions, during physical exercise, late at night, driving, in the company of others, etc.

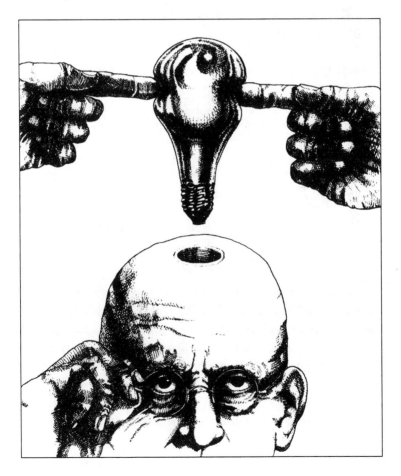

I have asked this question to many people. The answers I've received can be grouped into two categories. The first is "necessity," and it is represented by replies such as:

"When I'm faced with a problem."

"When things break down, and I have to fix them."

"When there's a need to be filled."

"When the deadline is near . . . that's the ultimate inspiration."

These responses bear out the old adage that "necessity is the *mother* of invention." But interestingly enough, an equal if not greater number of people get their ideas in the opposite situation, and they respond along these lines:

"When I'm just playing around."

"When I'm doing something else."

"When I'm not taking myself seriously."

"After my second beer."

From this I conclude that necessity may be the mother of invention, but play is certainly the *father*. As we said in the opening chapter, a playful attitude is fundamental to creative thinking. I'll bet that you generate most of your new ideas when you're playing in your mental playground. That's because your defenses are down, your mental locks are loosened, and there is little concern with the rules, practicality, or being wrong. When you play, you give yourself a license to try different approaches without fear of penalty.

Speaking of play, how did you do with the "squares" exercise at the beginning of this chapter? What ideas did you have? Population density chart? Maze constructed by a psychotic? Farmland from 35,000 feet? Tile floor? Nesting cubes? Television test pattern? These are all good imaginative descriptions of the squares. However, if you give yourself a license to play with the problem, you might try turning the problem upside down, and standing back about 10 meters. If you do this, you'll find that you no longer see the squares, but rather something much different — a picture of Abraham Lincoln.

Some people, however, think that if you're just playing at something, then you're really not working on it. Their attitude is, "Stop playing games and get down to business." They view work and play as two mutually exclusive boxes, and if you aren't producing hard tangible results, then you aren't working. They feel, in other words, that "play is frivolous." That's too bad, because these people are denying themselves all the good ideas they're entitled to.

A computer architect I know has this to say about play:

Play is what I do for a living.
The work comes in
organizing the results of the play.

He realizes that there are two sides to the creative process. The play side allows him to experiment with various approaches in order to learn what works and what doesn't and to take this knowledge to generate new ideas. The work side enables him to take what he has learned, evaluate it, corroborate it with existing knowledge, and to put it into a useful form.

One of play's products is fun — one of the most powerful motivators around. I've noticed that a fun working environment is significantly more productive than a routine environment. People who enjoy what they do will come up with more ideas. The fun is contagious, and everybody works harder to get a piece of it.

One woman told me that one of her keys to success is playfulness. "Whenever we hire new people, we're not concerned with how intelligent or efficient they are. To me the important characteristics are their playfulness and intensity. When people have these two traits, they're enthusiastic — and these are the ones who generate new ideas." (Note: the Greek word *enthousiasmos* means "the God within you." Enthusiastic people seem to have access to a spirit that serves as their source of inspiration.)

Some of the most important inventions and ideas were originally conceived for the purpose of play — their practical value to be discovered later. An example of this is the Moebius strip, a one-sided surface that has many unexpected properties. This topological idea was discovered by the German mathematician Augustus F. Moebius.

You can make a Moebius strip by taking a strip of paper and making a loop out of it. But before connecting the two ends, give one of them a half-twist. This loop now has only one side. You can prove this to yourself by taking a pencil and drawing a line all the way around the loop. Soon you will come back to your starting point. You will have covered the entire loop, thus proving that it has only one side. (It also has only one edge!)

Now take a pair of scissors and cut the strip along the line you have just drawn. What happens? Most loops, when cut in half, form two smaller loops. But this isn't so with the Moebius strip — it becomes one loop twice as long (but now it has two sides and is no longer a Moebius strip). Now try cutting a Moebius strip into thirds. This produces another surprise: two intertwined loops, one a two-sided loop and the other a Moebius strip.

For years, the Moebius strip was considered to be the "plaything of topology" — a nice amusement but not much more. In the last forty years, however, some practical applications have been found for the Moebius strip. Rubber manufacturers have used the Moebius strip for conveyor belts. The belt lasts longer because both sides are actually one and receive equal wear. Electric engineers have found that a resistor with a twist bent back on itself performs its function more efficiently. A continuous loop in a cassette cartridge will play twice as long if it has a twist in it. Chemists are exploring ways of making molecules in the shape of the Moebius strip. When they split, they get bigger rather than smaller.

Twelve-Sided Fun

Everyone has a favorite mathematical idea. Mine is the twelve-sided geometrical solid, the dodecahedron. (It's one of only five regular solids — the others being the tetrahedron, the cube, the octohedron, and icosahedron. These are known as the **Platonic** solids.) Believe it or not, many of the ideas in this book were generated while I was constructing and playing with dodecahedra.

You can make your very own dodecahedron by copying the template on the next page onto a thick piece of paper or cardboard. Cut along the solid lines and fold along the dotted lines. Fold each triangular tab under the adjacent pentagon and tape (or glue) down. After a while, you'll have your own dodecahedron to play with. You might even think of various things to put on the different sides.

Since this book was first published, I have received a variety of different dodecahedron applications. One person turned it into a Christmas card celebrating the twelve days of Christmas which the recipient could then fold into a Christmas tree ornament. Another person put twelve different shaped doodles on it to stimulate her thinking. Still another person started a company that produces dodecahedra with advice for solving specific problems printed on the different faces.

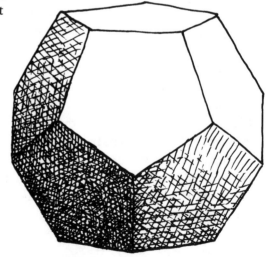

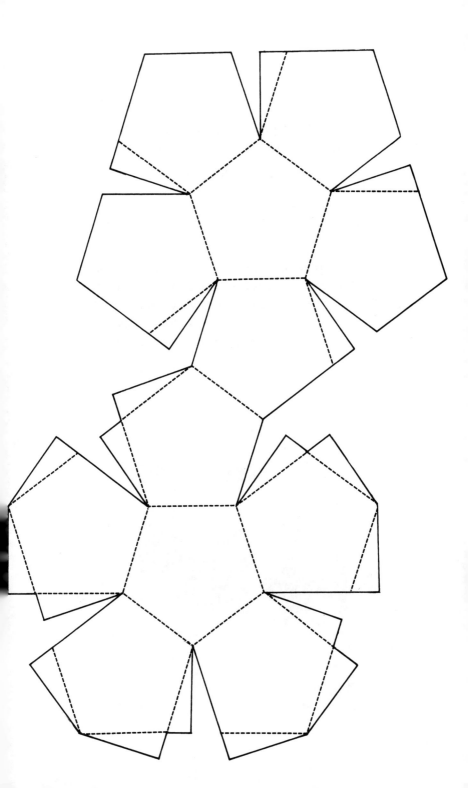

Pause for a Bit

Learn to pause . . . or nothing worthwhile will catch up to you.

— Doug King, Poet

Exercise: Take a minute and see if you can think of at least seven major cities that begin with the letter "M."

Playing is also a good way to get away from the problem you're working on. Indeed, sometimes pausing and turning the problem over to the active powers of your unconscious can be the best strategy of all. As software developer Rick Tendy put it, "I never try to solve a problem by trying to solve it."

By putting the idea on your mental back burner, you allow three beneficial things to take place. First, you put your problem in perspective. Sometimes we get so close to the problem that we lose sight of what we're trying to accomplish. One advertising man told me that his strategy for coming up with ideas is to spend five or six weeks inundating himself with information about the client and its market. Then he'll go fishing for three days, and "let the ideas percolate their way to the top." To draw an analogy to the Lincoln exercise you just did, we spend most of our time "thinking in the squares." But, if you allow yourself to back away to incubate, then you'll see the big picture.

Second, when you work on a problem, you plant a seed in your mind. When you back away, this seed continues to grow. It sends its roots out in your gray matter and makes new connections. For example, how did you do with the cities that begin with "M" exercise? That wasn't too difficult. You probably immediately thought of such cities as Miami, Montreal, Munich, Minneapolis, Marseilles, Melbourne, and Madrid. But now that the problem has been planted in your mind, when you wake up tomorrow morning you'll think of seven more (Memphis, Minsk, Mazatlan, Moscow, Mexico City, Mecca, and Montevideo), and continue to think — at least unconsciously — of more after that (Managua, Manila, Madras, Mombasa, Maracaibo, Milan, and Marrakech . . .).

Third, when you return to an idea or problem after incubating, you'll approach it with somewhat different assumptions. An engineering vice president told me that his advice to his employees is:

One o'clock should mean something new.

Some of his people spend all of their time focusing directly on the problem. They'll work on it all morning, and when noon comes, they'll bring out their bag lunches and continue to work on it. At one o'clock, they continue to work on it, and as a result, they bring no fresh perspective to the problem. The vice president encourages his people to go to lunch, exercise, play chess, go to the library — anything to break set.

One last note on incubation: sometimes delaying action will give you more information. Designer Christopher Williams tells the following story about an architect who built a cluster of large office buildings that were set in a central green. When construction was completed, the landscape crew asked him where he wanted the sidewalks between the buildings. "Not yet," was the architect's reply, "just plant the grass solidly between the buildings." This was done, and by late summer the new lawn was laced with pathways of trodden grass, connecting building to building. As Williams puts it, "The paths followed the most efficient line between the points of connection, turned in easy curves rather than right angles, and were sized according to traffic flow. In the fall, the architect simply paved the pathways. Not only did the pathways have a design beauty, they responded directly to user needs."

Summary

If necessity is the mother of invention, play is the father. Use it to fertilize your thinking.

TIP: The next time you have a problem, play with it.

TIP: If you don't have a problem, take time to play anyway. You may find some new ideas.

6. That's Not My Area

The Solar Cell

A solar energy lab technician has a problem. Her research lab is experimenting with a solar cell material, gallium arsenide, which is causing her problems in the slicing stage of cell production. Her task is to use a special high-speed wafer saw to make precision cuts in the material. But every time she cuts the material it cracks. She tries changing the position of the saw. The material still cracks. She is quite frustrated.

At home that weekend, she is in her husband's shop watching him make cabinets. She notices that when he wants to make precision cuts on certain types of wood, he reduces (rather than increases) the saw's cutting speed. She gets an idea: why not try the same approach on the gallium arsenide. She does, and it works.

What this woman did exemplifies an important part of creative thinking: recognizing the basic idea of one situation and applying it to another. The benefits of transferring knowledge gained in one area to another seem obvious. Why don't people do it more often?

One answer is specialization. As a strategy for managing information, specialization is essential. There is so much going on that it's impossible to pay attention to everything. Each second our nervous system is bombarded by approximately 100,000 bits of information. If we responded to that much information, our nervous systems would snap. It would be like a clam trying to siphon up all the sludge in San Francisco Bay — it just can't be done. Thus, one benefit of specialization is that it allows us to reduce the amount of irrelevant and trivial outside information we take in.

Similarly, as a strategy for getting along in the world, specialization is a necessity. In order to be effective in most endeavors — education, business, sports, technology, cooking — you have to narrow your area and become an expert. Look at baseball. It used to be that relief pitchers were used sparingly; the starters were expected to go all the way. Now there is a whole array of specialized relievers: long relievers, intermediate relievers, short relievers, relievers who throw smoke to right-handed batters, etc. Look at the variety of different types of accountants: tax specialists, management specialists, estate planning specialists, audit specialists, and so on.

The more complicated things become, the higher the walls go between the specialties. When I was in graduate school, I knew a marine biologist who was unable to talk with a molecular biologist because of the specialized nature of their disciplines. So, we have a situation where people know more and more about less and less.

That's Not My Area

As a strategy for creative thinking, specialization is dangerous because it can lead to the attitude "that's not my area." When this happens, a person may not only delimit her problems to too small an area, she may also stop looking for ideas in other fields.

How many times have you heard someone say, "That's an administration problem," "That's a marketing problem," or "That's an engineering problem"? We hear it all the time. Very few problems, however, are pure engineering problems. Most are engineering and manufacturing problems — and perhaps even marketing problems. Most computer problems are not only computer problems, but also communications and finance problems. But if a person thinks, "that's not my area," she won't be defining the problem in such broad terms.

Here is an example of some of the consequences of this attitude. One of my manufacturing clients had a "single-sourced" capacitor designed into a circuit-board his company was producing. Manufacturing people typically go out of their way to avoid single-sourced parts, i.e., those produced by only one outside vendor. They reason that if only one vendor is producing a particular sub-component, then an entire manufacturing group can be idled if anything happens to the vendor's capability to produce.

Things were fine until the vendor had production problems and could no longer meet demand. My client spent a lot of time attempting to track down more capacitors, but was unsuccessful. Finally, he went back through five layers of management to the design department to see how critical this capacitor was, and if it would be possible to use a replacement. When the design engineer was asked why this particular capacitor had been chosen, he replied, "I chose it because it's blue, and it looks good on the circuit board." The designer had never bothered to consider what impact such a choice would actually have on getting the product out the door. His tunnel-vision had prevented him from even looking for such a problem.

Cross-Fertilization

I have worked with the movie and television industries, the advertising profession, high technology research groups, packaged goods groups, hospital and health care professionals, and art departments. The one common denominator I have found is that each culture feels that it is the most creative, and that its members have a special elixir for new ideas. I think this is nice. *Esprit de corps* helps to create a good working environment. But I also feel that television people could learn a lot from elementary school teachers, and that research and development could pick up a few ideas from advertising. Every culture, industry, discipline, department, and organization has its own metaphors, models, methodologies, and short cuts for dealing with problems. But often the best ideas come from cutting across disciplinary boundaries and looking into other fields for new ideas. Many significant advances in art, business, education, entertainment, politics, and science have come about through a cross-fertilization of ideas. And to give a corollary, nothing will make a field stagnate more quickly than keeping out foreign ideas.

Here are a few examples of how people have taken ideas from one field and used them to make discoveries in another:

◆ An aerospace manager told me that he took up the hobby of designing and constructing backyard waterfalls for himself and his friends. "I don't know why," he said, "but designing waterfalls has made me a better manager. It has brought me a lot closer in touch with concepts such as *flow, movement,* and *vibration.* These concepts are difficult to put into words, but they are important in communicating between two people."

◆ I read about a birth control device developed by a gynecologist collaborating with a dentist. An unusual combination! We'd expect the gynecologist — who else specializes in female anatomy? But the dentist? The dentist, however, makes much of his living working with forms, shapes, and molds.

◆ The real estate entrepreneur Frank Morrow explains that he got his entrepreneurial education while attending the Graduate School of Business at Stanford — but not in the usual way. "I took all of the required courses in marketing, finance, accounting, and so on, but I learned more about business from a drawing course taught by the artist Nathan Olivera. What Olivera taught was: 'All art is a series of recoveries from the first line. The hardest thing to do is to put down the first line. But you must.' The same is true in business. You must act. A lot of business school types analyze things to death and never get around to acting. Perhaps more of them should take drawing courses."

◆ I once asked computer entrepreneur Steve Jobs why some people are more creative than others. He replied, "Innovation is usually the result of connections of past experience. But if you have the same experiences as everybody else, you're unlikely to look in a different direction. For example, I went to Reed College in Portland. At Reed, most of the men took modern dance classes from a woman named Judy Massey. We did it to meet the women. I didn't realize how much I learned about movement and perception from that class until a few years later when I worked for Nolan Bushnell at Atari. I was able to relate how much resolution of movement you need in terms of perceiving things for video games."

Exercise: "Most advances in science," explains physicist Peter Borden, "come when a person is forced to change fields." You can "change fields" briefly by taking someone to lunch. Let's suppose that the following pairs of people went to lunch together. What could they learn from one another?

➡ A bus driver and a comedian.

➡ A beautician and an insurance salesman.

➡ A kindergarten teacher and a software programmer.

➡ A priest and the head waiter at a fancy restaurant.

➡ A nurse in a cancer ward and a jazz drummer.

➡ A choreographer and a bookie.

➡ A prostitute and a professional football player.

➡ A policeman and a librarian.

➡ A circus clown and an air traffic controller.

➡ A bull fighter and a gardener.

➡ A fool and a banker.

Be An Explorer

**Anyone can look for fashion in a
boutique or history in a museum.
The creative person looks for history in
an airport and fashion in an airport.**

— Robert Wieder, Journalist

It's one thing to be open to new ideas; it's quite another to go on the offensive and actively seek them out. I encourage you to be an "explorer" and search for ideas outside your area. A good explorer knows that looking for good ideas is like prospecting for gold. If you look in the same old places, you'll find tapped out veins. But if you venture off the beaten path, you'll improve your chances of discovering new idea lodes.

To be an explorer you must believe that there is a lot of good information around you, and all you have to do is find it. If you go to an airport, you'll find ideas there. If you go to a museum, you'll find ideas there as well. And the same applies to hardware stores, garbage dumps, boutiques, libraries, parking garages, wilderness areas, restaurants, botanical gardens, and classrooms. Indeed, the more divergent your sources, the more original the idea you create is likely to be.

Many good ideas have been discovered because someone poked around in an outside industry or discipline, and applied what he found to his own field. World War I military designers borrowed from the cubist art of Picasso and Braque to create more efficient camouflage patterns for tanks and guns. Football coach Knute Rockne got the idea for his "four horsemen" backfield shift while watching a burlesque chorus routine. Mathematician John von Neumann analyzed poker-table behavior and developed the "game theory" model of economics. The roll-on deodorant was an adaptation of the ball-point pen. Drive-in banks were adapted from drive-in restaurants. I've known songwriters who got inspiration from listening to crowd chants at basketball games, venture capitalists who spotted new opportunities by going to junkyards, educators who got ideas by going to prisons, advertising people who borrowed ideas from biology, and software programmers who were influenced by songwriters. It's not surprising that Thomas Edison gave his colleagues this advice:

Make it a point to keep on the lookout for novel and interesting ideas that others have used successfully. Your idea has to be original only in its adaptation to the problem you are currently working on.

Exercise: Where do you explore for ideas? What outside people, places, activities, and situations do you use to stimulate your thinking? I've asked many people this question. Here are some of their answers.

Magic. Through the study and performance of magic, I've learned the power that certain symbols have when they are associated with one another. I've taken this knowledge and applied it to sales and product demonstrations.

Junkyards. Going to a junkyard is a sobering experience. There you can see the ultimate destination of almost everything we desire.

Acting Class. From acting class I have been able to appreciate the impact that positive encouragement has on a person. I have seen some performances that were so bad that I was embarrassed to watch. But the acting coach gave the person criticism in an encouraging way. As a result, these people were able to grow as actors. I think that there is a lesson here for many areas of life.

Old Science Magazines. I get ideas from reading old popular science magazines from the early twentieth century. There were many good ideas proposed then that couldn't be implemented because the materials weren't available. However, the materials to implement them are available now.

History. History is filled with examples. Napoleon marching on Moscow is really just project management. Mao carrying on a guerrilla war is like launching an advertising campaign.

Exercise: Nature is a great place to explore for ideas. Think about it, in the course of their evolution, natural systems have solved a variety of problems — often in quite ingenious ways. Bionics is a field of engineering in which ideas from natural systems are "borrowed" and then adapted for human uses. Listed below are some examples of this. See if you can connect each specimen with its subsequent engineering application.

Specimen	Engineering Application
1. Elm tree seeds: "wing structure"	**A.** Device for detecting poisonous mine gases
2. Fly: vertical takeoff	**B.** Infrared photography
3. Salmon: organ for detecting extremely dilute solutions of odoriferous liquid	**C.** Improved windmill design; safer helicopters
4. Burdock burr: hooked spines	**D.** Fiberglass-reinforced plastics
5. Moth: antenna is olfactory organ of high sensitivity	**E.** Reliable celestial compass
6. Snake: thermoscopic vision that detects 0.002° C. temperature gradient	**F.** Device for detecting pollutants in water
	G. Vertical takeoff aircraft
7. Bamboo stalk: two-phase composite fiber construction	**H.** Improved hydrophone design
8. Beehive: hexagonal construction	**I.** Basis for a commercial fastener
9. Bee eyes: segment facets filter polarized light	**J.** Stronger and lighter pool tables
10. Seals: hearing apparatus for underwater sound detection	

Summary

Specialization is a fact of life. In order to function in the world, you have to narrow your focus and limit your field of view. When you're trying to generate new ideas, however, such information-handling attitudes can limit you. They not only may force you into delimiting your problem too narrowly, they may also prevent you from looking in outside areas for ideas.

TIP: Develop the explorer's attitude: the outlook that wherever you go, there are ideas waiting to be discovered.

TIP: Don't get so busy that you lose the free time necessary for exploring. Give yourself a non-task day once a month or so, or an afternoon every several weeks. When was the last time you went to a junkyard? A sporting event? A television studio? Schedule exploring time into your day and week.

TIP: When you "capture" an idea, be sure to write it down.

TIP: Sometimes the most helpful ideas are right in front of us. As the noted explorer Scott Love once put it, "Only the most foolish of mice would hide in a cat's ear. But only the wisest of cats would think to look there." Don't miss the obvious. Ask yourself: "What resources and solutions are right in front of me? What am I overlooking?"

7. Don't Be Foolish

Going Along

The nail that sticks up
will be hammered down.

— Japanese Proverb

Scene #1. A man walks into the waiting room of a doctor's office. He looks around and is surprised by what he sees: everybody is in their underwear. People are drinking coffee in their underwear, reading magazines in their underwear, and carrying on conversations in their underwear. He's shocked at first, but then decides that they must know something he doesn't. After twenty seconds, he too takes off his clothes and sits down in his underwear.

Scene #2. A woman waits patiently for an elevator in an office building. After a short period, the elevator arrives and the doors open. As she looks in, she notices that everybody is turned around and facing to the rear of the elevator. So, she, too, gets into the elevator and faces the rear.

These scenes are from Allen Funt's 1960's television series *Candid Camera.* They both confirm what countless psychology tests have found, namely, the best way to get along is to go along.

All of us are subject to group pressures. Study your own behavior, and you'll see how much you conform to various situations. Let's suppose that you're driving down the freeway, and everyone around you is going ten miles per hour over the speed limit. What happens? It's very difficult not to break the law — you get caught up in the "flow of traffic." Suppose that you are a pedestrian standing at the corner of an intersection in a major city. Ten or twelve other people are standing there with you. The sign says, "DON'T WALK," but no traffic is coming. Then one of the pedestrians crosses the street against the light. Soon another goes, and then another. In no time, all the other pedestrians have crossed the street against the light. And you do too, because you would feel really stupid being the only person still standing there.

Let's suppose you're in a check-out line at a grocery store. The other people in line are standing silently facing the cash register. What do you do? Do you tell them about your theory of the tripartite nature of the soul? Do you ask them what their favorite colors are? Do you start making chicken noises? No, you look straight ahead and keep your mouth shut because that's what people do in checkout lines. After all, you don't want to look foolish, do you?

Benefits of Conformity

Conformity serves several practical purposes. First, living in society requires your cooperation with other people. Without conformity, traffic would get tied up, production quotas would be missed, and the fabric of society would come apart. Part of the price you pay for the benefits of your social existence is a piece of your own individuality. There are hundreds, if not thousands, of rituals you go through in which your behavior must conform to the people around you — everything from how you pronounce words so that you effectively communicate to driving on the proper side of the road to assure smooth traffic flow. If you don't conform, not only might you throw a monkey wrench in the gears of society, you also run the risk of appearing stupid — like you don't know what's going on.

Second, in those situations where you don't know your way around, what do you do? You look to others for the right way to act. Suppose you're in a laundromat, and you're not quite sure how to operate the washing machine. What do you do? Probably look over to the person next to you and try the approach that person is using. Similarly, I once watched my then four year old son view a *Three Stooges* movie. For the most part, he sat silently trying to figure out what was going on. The next day, when he watched the movie with his seven year old sister, he laughed at all the same places she did. In this way, he was developing a sophisticated sense of humor.

My favorite example of conformity is a story about Saint Augustine. As a young priest in Milan, he went to his bishop, Ambrose, for help with a problem. It seemed that Augustine was going to spend the weekend in Rome. His problem was that in Rome it was customary to celebrate the Sabbath on Sunday, while in Milan it was celebrated on Saturday. Augustine was confused as to which was the right day. Ambrose solved Augustine's problem by telling him:

When in Rome, do as the Romans do.

Groupthink

New ideas, however, are not born in a conforming environment. Whenever people get together, there is the danger of "groupthink." This is the phenomenon in which group members are more interested in getting the approval of the others rather than trying to come up with creative solutions to the problems at hand. Thus, when everyone thinks alike, no one is doing very much thinking.

Alfred Sloan knew the dangers of groupthink. In the late 1930's, he was chairing a board meeting at General Motors. An idea was proposed, and everybody became enthusiastic about it. One person said, "We'll make a lot of money with this proposal." Another said, "Let's implement it as soon as possible." And still another said, "We'll bury competition." After the discussion, Sloan said, "It's now time to vote on the proposal." The vote went around the table, and each board member voted "Aye." When the vote came back to Sloan, he said, "I, too, vote 'Aye' and that makes it unanimous. And for that reason, I'm going to table the motion until next month. I don't like what's happening to our thinking. We're getting locked into looking at this idea in just one way, and this is a dangerous way to make decisions. I want each of you to spend the next month studying this proposal from a different perspective." A month went by, and the proposal was brought up again. This time, however, it was voted down. The board members had had an opportunity to break through the effects of groupthink.

Similarly, I remember in the 1970's visiting my cousin, a farmer, in North Dakota. He showed me a freshly constructed pig cellar for breeding pigs. It was beautiful. I asked him if he was happy about it. He replied, "I would be except that the building inspector told me that everywhere he goes he sees people putting in pig cellars. That means that in eighteen months there will be a glut and prices will go down." Sure enough, a year and a half later, prices for his pork products plummeted.

Consult A Fool

Any decision-maker (and we all are) has to deal with the problem of conformity and groupthink. But how? Why not do what decision-makers and problem-solvers since the dawn of civilization have done to stimulate their imaginations and improve their judgment:

Ask a fool what he thinks.

Looking at the fool's wildly-colored clothing and donkey-eared cap, it's easy to regard him as a simpleton, an imbecile whose proverbial "elevator doesn't go all the way to the top floor," or a moron "whose bell has no clapper." Don't be fooled! The classical fool is no dunce. It takes intelligence, imagination, cleverness, and insight to play this role. A good fool needs to be part actor and part poet, part philosopher and part psychologist.

The fool was consulted by Egyptian pharaohs and Babylonian kings. His opinion was sought by Roman emperors and Greek tyrants. He advised Indian chiefs in the Pueblo, Zuni, and Hopi nations. He played an important role at the courts of the Chinese emperors. The fool was prominently employed by European royalty in the Middle Ages and Renaissance. Because of his ability to open up people's thinking, the fool has been held in as much esteem as the priest, the medicine man, and the shaman.

What did the fool do? Simply stated, it was his job to whack the king's (pharaoh, emperor, chief, decision-maker, problem-solver, etc.) thinking out of habitual thought patterns. The king's advisers were often "yes-men" — they told him exactly what he wanted to hear. The king realized that this wasn't a good way to make decisions. Therefore, he gave the fool a license to parody any proposal under discussion and to shatter the prevailing mindset. The fool's candid jokes and offbeat observations put the issue in a fresh light and forced the king to re-examine his assumptions. By listening to the fool, the king improved his judgment, enhanced his creativity, and protected himself from groupthink.

The fool operates in a world that runs counter to conventional patterns. Everyday ways of perceiving, understanding, and acting have little meaning for him. He'll extol the trivial, trifle the exalted, and parody the common perception of a situation. Here are some examples of the fool's approach:

The fool will reverse our standard assumptions. He might say, "If a man is sitting on a horse facing the rear, why do we assume that it is the man who is backwards and not the horse?"

He is irreverant. He'll pose a riddle such as: "What is it that the rich man puts in his pocket that the poor man throws away?" When he answers, "Snot," he forces you to re-examine the sanctity of your most basic daily rituals.

He might deny that a problem even exists and thus reframe the situation. Most people think recessions are bad. Not the fool. The fool says, "Recessions are good. They make people work more efficiently. People work harder when they are insecure about the future of their jobs. Also, most companies have a fair amount of fat in them. Recessions force them to trim back to their fighting weight and be more aggressive."

The fool can be absurd. Having lost his donkey, a fool got down on his knees and began thanking God. A passerby saw him and asked, "Your donkey is missing; what are you thanking God for?" The fool replied, "I'm thanking Him for seeing to it that I wasn't riding him at the time. Otherwise, I would be missing too."

The fool notices things that other people overlook. He might ask, "Why do people who pour cream into their coffee do so after the coffee is already in the cup, rather than pouring the cream in first and saving themselves the trouble of stirring?"

The fool is metaphorical. When answering the following question on an intelligence test: "Which is true: A) Birds eat seeds, or B) Seeds eat birds," he might answer both A and B because he has seen dead birds on the ground decompose into the soil to fertilize freshly planted seeds.

The fool will apply the rules of one arena to a different one. He'll go to a football game and imagine he's in church. He'll see the players huddling and think they're praying. He'll see the vendors in the stands and think that they're taking up a collection. He'll see the fans' hero worship of the star quarterback and imagine that he's witnessing the Second Coming.

The fool can be cryptic. He'll say the best way to see something is with your ears. Initially, this may seem a little weird, but after you've thought about it, you just might agree that *listening* to a poem or a story conjures up more images in your mind than *watching* television.

Physicist Niels Bohr felt that thinking like a fool was essential to coming up with breakthrough ideas. During a tense brainstorming session, he told a colleague:

We all know your idea is crazy. The question is, whether it is crazy enough?

The great benefit of the fool's antics and observations is that they stimulate your thinking. They jolt your mind in the same way that a splash of cold water wakes you up when you're drowsy.

You may not like the fool's ideas. Some of them may even irritate you or strike you as silly or useless. But he forces you to entertain — perhaps only momentarily — an alternative way of looking at your situation. Whatever assumptions you hold must be suspended. The fool's approach to life jars you into an awareness that there is a second right answer to what you're doing, and that you should look for better answers than the ones you've got. Indeed, sometimes the fool makes more sense than the wise man. In a time when things are changing very quickly, who is to say what's right and what's foolish. As Albert Einstein once said:

An idea that sometimes drives me hazy: Am I or are the others crazy?

Indeed, sometimes the fool makes more sense than the wise man. Some of the most foolish ideas from five years ago are now a reality.

Put On Your Fool's Cap

**If anyone among you thinks he is
wise in this age, let him become a fool
that he may become wise.**

— I Corinthians 3:18

What if you don't have a fool around to help you? Why not give yourself a license to be foolish. You're smart, right? You've got a sense of humor, right? Go ahead and put on your fool's cap. You will find that it cleanses your judgment and opens up your mind. Don't worry about people who say "don't be foolish." After all, you know that thinking like a fool is for a good purpose. Dig into your fool's bag of tricks. Look at the problem before you and say, "It's not what everyone thinks it is," and give a different interpretation of what's going on. Deny that the problem even exists, or maybe solve a different one. Doubt the things that others take for granted. Ridicule your basic assumptions. Expect the unexpected. Ask the stupid question that nobody else seems to be asking. Do whatever you can to shatter the established way of looking at things. You'll find that it will stimulate your creative juices.

Remember those situations when you put on your fool's cap? What happened? Did you come up with a lot of different ideas? Were you more creative? Did you take more risks? Did you have more fun? I'm sure that the answer to all of these questions is "yes." From my own experience I've found that the most effective creative thinking sessions I've conducted were those in which the participants allowed themselves to be foolish.

Here are several of the fool's favorite tools.

Laugh at It

As soon as you have made a thought, laugh at it.

— Lao Tzu, Philosopher

The fool believes that if you can laugh at something — be it a problem, a project, a recipe for chicken, how airplanes are designed, or your relationship with another person — then you're more likely to think about it in a fresh way. Laughter puts you at ease. Do you feel more comfortable talking with someone who has just told you a joke, or with someone who is deadly serious? Would you rather listen to a speaker who approaches his subject in a plodding straightforward manner or one who has just given you a humorous aside on the state of your business?

Getting into a humorous frame of mind not only loosens you up, it enhances your creativity. This has been demonstrated in tests investigating the role humor plays in stimulating a creative outlook. Typically the tests are run as follows: test participants are divided into two equal groups. One group sits silently in a study hall for a half an hour prior to the test. The other group spends the same time in another room listening to an audio tape of a standup comedian telling jokes like:

Question: How deep is the ocean?
Answer: Just a stone's throw.

Question: What do John the Baptist and Winnie the Pooh have in common?
Answer: They both have the same middle name.

Question: What do you get when you combine the Godfather with a lawyer?
Answer: An offer you can't understand.

Then both groups take the creativity test. The group that's involved in the comedy usually does much better. The comedy loosens up their thinking and establishes an environment in which people can be creative.

Why is this? First, humor stretches your thinking. The term "just a stone's throw" typically denotes a short distance. But when you throw a rock into water, it travels until it reaches the bottom — perhaps as much as seven miles depending on where you toss it. The punch line forces you to make a shift in how you think about a "stone's throw." Getting the joke then is an exercise in "breaking set" — one of the key aspects of "thinking something different." For if a stone's throw can mean *seven miles,* who is to stop you from looking at a broken light bulb as a *knife,* a vacuum cleaner as a *musical instrument,* snails as *food,* a clothespin as a *toy,* a potato as a *radio antenna,* or a box of packaged baking soda as *refrigerator deodorant?*

Secondly, humor forces you to combine ideas that are usually not associated with one another. Few people think of "John the Baptist" and "Winnie the Pooh" as having much in common. The former was a first century Jewish prophet who baptized Jesus; the latter a frivolous fictional bear created nineteen centuries later by the English poet A.A. Milne. Yet for purposes of this joke, this unlikely pair is brought together. In a world where John the Baptist and Winnie the Pooh can be thrown together into one concept, what's to stop you from combining television sets and flea repellent into one idea? Or sunglasses and prayer meetings? Or freeway congestion and bookmarks? If you think hard enough, you'll think of a connection. This type of thinking is also at the core of creativity. The ancients combined soft copper with even softer tin to create hard bronze. The first person to put a satellite dish on the back of a truck to create a mobile uplink-downlink station did this. So did the person who combined a surfboard and a sail to create the sport of windsurfing. So did the person who combined movies and airplanes to create in-flight entertain-

ment. I'm sure you can think of many other creations that were the combination of simple ideas.

Third, humor allows you to take things less seriously. In the Godfather-lawyer joke, both attorneys and Mafia Dons are targeted. Just how effective would a Godfather be if he couldn't threaten people? How effective would an attorney be if he couldn't find and create loopholes? If you can make fun of something, then you're more likely to challenge the rules that give that "something" its legitimacy, and perhaps you can think of alternatives.

This is not meant to be a treatise on humor. (Heaven knows! Some of the most boring works around are those describing humor.) But the point is this: there is a close relationship between the "haha" of humor and the "aha!" of discovery. If you employ the same thinking that you use in humor — breaking set, putting ideas into different new contexts, seeking ambiguity, combining different ideas, asking unusual "what if" questions, parodying the rules — and apply it to problem-solving, then you're likely to come up with some fresh approaches to what you're working on.

Humor may not solve your problem, but it will put you in a more conducive mood to do so. From my own experience conducting creativity workshops, I've found that humor works wonders to stimulate the flow of ideas. If, early on in a session, I encourage the participants to be humorous in their approach to the problem, their answers are usually much more interesting and provocative. Not only that, they're more candid in their approach to the more serious issues that I subsequently present to them. The corollary to this is that if I don't use humor early on, the people are likely to sit on their hands and be judgmental. Here's my advice:

Go ahead and be whacky. Get into a crazy frame of mind and ask what's funny about what you're doing.

Humor is an effective tool even with the gravest of problems. As the physicist Niels Bohr once put it, "There are some things that are so serious that you have to laugh at them." Some people are so closely married to their ideas that they put them up on a pedestal. It's difficult to be creative when you have that much ego tied up in your idea. Therefore, step back, loosen up, and remember Laroff's credo:

It's not so important to be
serious as it is to be serious
about the important things.
The monkey wears an
expression of seriousness
that would do credit to any
great scholar. But the monkey
is serious because he itches.

Reverse Your Viewpoint

You can't see the good ideas behind you by looking twice as hard at what's in front of you.

— Andrew Mercer, Innovator

In the late 1950's, a mysterious phenomenon occurred in Seattle: people began discovering small pockmarks on their car windshields. As more and more of these tiny indented scars were found, a kind of mass hysteria developed. Two main theories arose to explain the cause of the pitting. One was that atomic tests by the Russians had contaminated the atmosphere, and this, combined with Seattle's moist climate, had produced

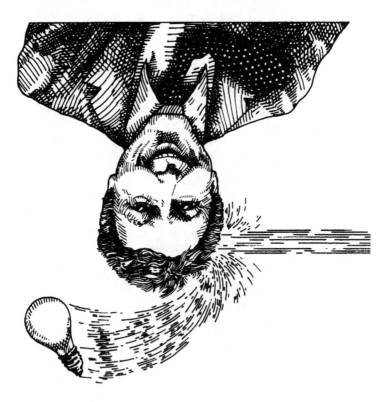

fallout that was returning to earth in a glass-etching dew. The other theory was that Seattle's recently constructed roads, again with the help of the foggy dew, were flinging acid drops against the windshields. As the situation became more serious, the Federal government sent a team of experts to investigate the mystery. What they discovered was that there was *no increase* in windshield pitting at all. As the reports of the windshield pits came to the attention of more and more people, they began to check their own cars. Most did this by looking through the glass from the outside of the car instead of from the inside. This revealed the pitting that is almost invariably caused by normal wear on a windshield. What had broken out was an epidemic not of windshield pitting, but of *reverse windshield viewing.* People reversed their view of the windshield and discovered something that had always been there but they'd never noticed.

This story illustrates what can happen when you reverse your point of view. The fool believes that thinking about and doing things opposite from your customary way allows you to discover the things you typically overlook. For example, when everyone else is gazing at a gorgeous sunset, why not turn around to see the blues and violets behind you? What do you notice when you look at a coffee cup? Its color? Its material? Its design? Reverse your focus and look at the empty space inside the cup. Isn't that what gives it its functional value?

When you look at a lawn just after it's been mowed, what do you typically think about? That it looks nice and neat? That it has a fresh smell? How about reversing your viewpoint and paying attention to where the grass clippings have gone? What problems do they create? What other uses could you make of them? Compost pile? Land fill? Stuffing?

Reversing your perspective is a good technique for opening up your thinking. Here's an example of how such a strategy can work. Carl Djerassi, one of the developers of the birth control pill in the 1950's, is the head of a pesticide company. As such, he's concerned about the adverse health and economic effects that certain insects have on society. Like many other scientists, he's also concerned about the harmful side-effects that many pesticides have on the environment. He asks himself, "How can I eliminate harmful insects without harming the environment?" He plays with his objective and decides to focus not on *death* but on *birth.* "What if rather than killing the insects we prevented them from being born in the first place? If we gave them specially-targeted hormones that would prevent their sex organs from reaching maturity, they wouldn't be able to reproduce themselves." He tries it, and it works.

Doing the opposite of what's expected can also be an effective strategy in competitive situations such as sports, business, warfare, romance, etc. In most endeavors, we build up certain expectations about what the other side will or won't do. In football, for example, a third and one situation will typically cause the defense to prepare for a plunge into the line. In retailing, you can bet that stores will do a lot of advertising between Thanksgiving and Christmas. In politics, most candidates will have a last minute media blitz. In these situations, trends get established. When you do the opposite of what people are expecting, chances are good that you'll catch them off-guard and be more successful in reaching your objective.

Psychiatrist Paul Watzlawick tells the following delightful story in which doing the unexpected worked in a wartime situation. In 1334, the Duchess of Tyrol laid siege to the castle of Hochosterwitz in Austria. She knew that the siege would take some months because the fortress was located on a cliff high above the valley floor. As time wore on, the defenders in the castle became desperate; their only remaining food was an ox and several bags of grain. The Duchess's situation, however, had also become severe; her troops were becoming unruly, there seemed to be no end to the siege, and she had pressing matters elsewhere.

At this point, the castle's commander hit upon a plan of action that must have seemed utter lunacy to his men. He slaughtered the last ox, stuffed it with grain, and then threw the carcass over the cliff onto the meadow in front of the enemy camp. The Duchess interpreted this scornful message to mean that the castle had so much food they could afford to waste it. Because the castle's commander did the opposite of what the Duchess expected, he jolted her into believing that her siege wasn't working. Thereupon, the discouraged Duchess abandoned her siege and moved on.

Try switching your objective and going in the opposite direction. Suppose you're a teacher and you wonder, "How can I be less effective?" This would mean that the student would have to take more responsibility for her learning, and this could lead to the development of a self-study go-at-your-own-pace program.

Suppose you're a basketball coach and you ask, "How can I get my team out-of-sync?" Your answer might be a list of things that would unsettle them. Then you could practice these things, because they might have to deal with them in a game.

Suppose you're in a grocery store buying produce. You see people around you jamming lettuce, grapes, and broccoli into plastic bags. You ask yourself, "What if I did this backwards? What if I put my *hand* in the bag, and then grabbed the produce and pulled the bag over it?"

Reversing your viewpoint is a great way to sharpen your thinking. Try disagreeing with people with whose ideas, principles, and beliefs you usually agree. You may find that the opposite view makes more sense. If you don't have anyone handy to disagree with you, why not disagree with yourself? Play the fool and take the contrary position on common sense proverbs.

"If something's worth doing, it's worth doing well." If a thing's worth doing, it's okay to do it poorly. Otherwise, you'll never give yourself permission to be a beginner at a new activity. If you have to do well, then you'll prevent yourself from trying new things.

"A bird in the hand is worth two in the bush." Two in the bush are great. After all, everybody needs a dream. Without the "two in the bush" mentality, what would happen to risk-taking?

"A chain is no stronger than its weakest link." Weak links are wonderful! As a matter of fact, many systems have weak links designed into them. They're called "fuses." When a system gets overloaded, the fuse blows and saves the rest of the system. After all, which part do you want to break: the $50,000 piece or the 5¢ one?

Exercise: Take one of your favorite pieces of common sense and roast it. You might try some of the following:

1. Business before pleasure.
2. Every cloud has a silver lining.
3. Every dog has its day.
4. Don't put all your eggs in one basket.
5. Fight fire with fire.
6. Patience is a virtue.
7. Haste makes waste.
8. He who laughs last laughs best.
9. Curiosity killed the cat.
10. Beauty is only skin-deep.
11. You can't teach an old dog new tricks.
12. If at first you don't succeed, try, try, again.
13. As you make your bed, so you must sleep in it.
14. Look before you leap.
15. Too many cooks spoil the soup.

Looking at things in reverse can also be a good technique for discovering the comic side of things. Here's one fool's view of what would happen if we lived our lives backwards.

> Life is tough. It takes up all your time, all your weekends, and what do you get at the end of it? Death, a great reward. The life cycle is all backwards. You should die first, and get it out of the way. Then you live for twenty years in an old age home, and then get kicked out when you're too young. You get a gold watch and then you go to work. You work forty years until you're young enough to enjoy your retirement.
>
> You go to college and party until you're ready for high school. Then you go to grade school, you become a little kid, you play, you have no responsibilities, you become a little baby, you go back into the womb, you spend your last nine months floating, and you finish off as a gleam in somebody's eye.

The Fools and the Rules

Finally, the fool loves to parody the rules. In my seminars, I provide an opportunity for participants to do just that. We play a game called the "Fools and the Rules." It's easy to play. You take your holiest sacred cow and sacrifice it on the altar of foolishness. In a perverse sort of way, sometimes the fool makes more sense than the rule. Here are some examples:

RULE: "Always be polite on the telephone."

FOOL: "Are you kidding? Abusive behavior cuts down on phone time. It also gives our public relations department more work. It would eliminate the hold button on the telephone as well as lead to honest employee relationships. Finally, rude telephone manners could serve as an outlet for employee stress."

RULE: "Our company is 'Committed to Excellence.'"

FOOL: "How about 'committed to incompetence.' Think of the possibilities! We would have less development time, lower training costs, and no backlogs. Part shortages wouldn't halt production. Also, we'd improve our chances of reaching our design goals, and we wouldn't be afraid to try new ideas — after all, what would we have to lose? In the past we've been able to sell our products based on their technical merits. With mediocre products, we'd have to learn how to sell. We'd also have a larger market: there are more mediocre people in the world than excellent ones. But we'd be successful because: Nothing succeeds like mediocrity because everybody understands it so well."

RULE: "Always communicate through the proper chain of command so as not to surprise your boss."

FOOL: "That's a waste of time. After all, bosses like surprises — they're fun! This would remove any chance for preconceptions (and we all know that preconceptions get in the way of creative ideas). This would also demonstrate how much goes on without anyone knowing. In addition, you would be provided with a means of visibility because you'd continually be called on to the carpet."

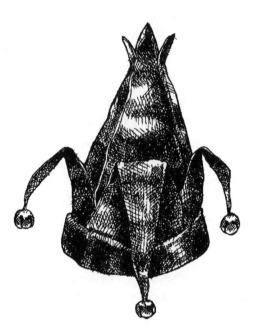

As you can see, playing the fool is a lot of fun. It's also a great way to generate ideas and examine your most basic assumptions. While the ideas produced may not be immediately useful, it may happen that a foolish idea will lead to a practical, creative idea. And if you come up empty, at least you'll understand why the rule was there in the first place.

Summary

The fool's job is to shake, assault, massage, caress, and take a whack at the habits, rules, and conventions that keep you thinking the same old stuff. A good way to think of the fool is to compare your thinking to the transmission of a car. Most of the gears, like most thinking, are designed to go forward, to get ahead, to get the job done. But sometimes, when you can't make forward progress, you need to put it in reverse so that you can go forward anew. That's what the fool is all about: he's the reverse gear for your mind! He may not give you the right answer or solve your problem, but he'll get you out of the rut and put your thinking on a mental freeway where you might find a better solution yourself.

TIP: Occasionally, let your "stupid monitor" down, play the fool, and see what crazy ideas you can come up with.

TIP: Reverse your perspective.* You'll see the things you usually don't look at. It's also a good way to free your thinking from deeply engrained assumptions. Example: Write two paragraphs describing a problem you're currently trying to solve. Here's the twist: if you're a male, write it from the viewpoint of a female; if you're a female, write it from a male's point of view. At the very least, you'll generate some interesting stepping stones.

TIP: Laugh at yourself. What are the funniest two things you've done in the past year? What did you learn?

---

*Of course, perceiving things backwards is not without its problems. The story goes that William Spooner (the late nineteenth century educator known for transposing the initial sounds of words, e.g., *tons of soil* for *sons of toil* or *queer old dean* for *dear old queen,* and from whom we get the term *Spoonerism*) was at a dinner party in which he happened to knock the salt shaker on the carpet. Without missing a beat, Spooner poured his wine on top of it.

8. Avoid Ambiguity

Thinking Ambiguously

Exercise: In the following line of letters, cross out six letters so that the remaining letters, without altering their sequence, will spell a familiar English word. Play with it for a while before proceeding.

B S A I N X L E A T N T E A R S

In the mid-1960's, FBI director J. Edgar Hoover was reading a typed copy of a letter he had just dictated to his secretary. He didn't like the way she had formatted the letter, so he wrote on the bottom, "Watch the borders," and asked her to retype it. The secretary did as she was instructed and sent it off to all top agents. For the next two weeks FBI agents were put out on special alert along the Canadian and Mexican borders.

This story illustrates two of the main reasons why most people don't like ambiguous situations (those that can be interpreted in more than one way): 1) they're confusing, and, 2) they cause communication problems. As a result, we have learned to "avoid ambiguity." This is a good rule to follow for most practical situations such as giving directions, documenting programs, or drawing up contracts. On these occasions it's important to be clear, precise, and specific in order to get your message across.

There are instances, however, when ambiguity can be a powerful stimulant to your imagination. When you're in the imaginative phase of the creative process, a little ambiguity can whack you into asking such questions as:

What's going on here?
What does this mean?
How else can this be interpreted?

These are special questions, the kind you ask when you are looking for new ideas. So, one way to "think something different" is to look at things ambiguously. For example, what is half of 8? One answer is 4. But if you assume that the question is ambiguous, you'll look for other answers such as 0, 3, E, M, and "eig," all depending on how you define "half."

Okay, how did you do with the six letters exercise? What word did you find? Many people look at the problem and say, "Okay, here's a string of sixteen letters, and to solve this problem I should cross out 6 of them. That means I'm looking for a 10 letter word." And that's what they spend their time looking for.

I gave this problem to a person who was an avid computer user. He went home that night and said, "I'll show that Roger. I'll write a program to cross out 6 letters, and have the computer figure out the answer. I'll just take a shower while it does this, and when I get back the answer will be printed out." When he came back, he had thirty pages of printout containing such glittering possibilities as:

SAINXEAEAR	BSAIXEEARS	BSINLEANEA
BINXLTEARS	AINXLEANAS	BANEATNTER
SINXEATNTE	BAINLATNAR	SNLETNTARS
SANLATNTAR	INXLEANEAR	INXEATEARS
BSNXLENTAT	INLETNTARS	SAIZNTEARS
SABXATNTEA	SINXLETERS	SAILTNTEAR
NLEATNTEAS	IXLEATNTAS	SAINLATEAR
SNXLETTARS	BSNLENEARS	INEATNTEAR
BSAXLETARS	BLEATTEARS	INXATNTEAR
BAINNEANTS	SXLEATNTES	BINLATTEAR

As soon as he saw the list, he realized that he had been asking the wrong question. He discovered that you could have the greatest computer on earth, but if you've got the wrong program in it, you'll end up with garbage.

One way to solve this problem is to interpret the instructions with an ambiguous attitude. What else could "cross out six letters" mean? Perhaps instead of crossing out 6 letters, you literally cross out the "S," and the "I," and the "X," and the "L," and the "E," and so on. If you try this approach, you will be left with the word:

B A N A N A

My point is this: one way to be more creative is to look for ambiguity in the world around you. The kindergartners who saw the chalk dot as an owl's eye, a cigar butt, a squashed bug had the ability to do this. So did Picasso when he saw the bicycle handlebars as bull's horns. So did Grace Hopper when she saw eleven inches of string as one nanosecond. And so have you if you've ever used a brick as a doorstop, made chimes out of forks and spoons, used leaves as toilet paper, or used a ball point pen as a hole punch. The ability to find ambiguity is an important part of "thinking something different."

The American General George S. Patton had similar ideas on how to stimulate people's creativity. He said, "If you tell people where to go, but not how to get there, you'll be amazed at the results." He knew that posing a problem in an ambiguous way would give more freedom to the imaginations of the people who were working on it.

The renowned Canadian architect Arthur Erickson uses this strategy to unlock his students' creativity. Here's an example of one of his exercises. Give it a try.

Note: Since this book is advocating looking for the second right answer, I should point out that there is at least one other solution to this problem. If you choose six different letters — say "B," "S," "A," "I," "N," and "X" — and cross them out every time they appear, you would end up with the word "LETTER."

Exercise: Draw a picture of yourself in a position of movement, and then provide a device (made out of plastic, wood, paper, or metal) to support that position.

At the end of the exercise, Erickson points out to his students that they have been designing furniture. As he puts it: "If I had said to the students, 'Look, we're going to design a chair or a bed,' they would have explored the design on the basis of previous memories of chairs and beds. But by approaching the model from the opposite and essential direction, I was able to make them realize the vital aspects of furniture."

As you can see, sometimes all you need is a dose or two of amibiguity to whack your thinking into high gear. Thus, I'd like to prescribe a few of the following sources of ambiguity to you.

Paradoxes

This chapter is paradoxical. On the one hand, I've said that ambiguity causes communications problems. On the other, I've said that it helps create new ideas. What's the common denominator? Both situations stimulate you to think.

That's probably the reason why, in the midst of a difficult problem, physicist Niels Bohr was overheard to say, "How wonderful that we've met with a paradox. Now we have hope of making some progress." Bohr knew that paradoxes are crucial to the creative process. That's because they whack you out of narrow thought paths and force you to question your assumptions. Indeed, the very act of "seeing the paradox" is at the crux of creative thinking — the ability to entertain two different, often contradictory, notions at the same time.

I'd like to share some of my favorites with you:

◆ The little I know I owe to my ignorance.
— *Orville Mars*

◆ There is nothing so unthinkable as thought unless it be the entire absence of thought.
— *Samuel Butler*

◆ Martie McKinney was disappointed to find no suggestion box in the clubhouse because she would like to put a suggestion in it about having one.
— *Judy Heller*

◆ Any company large enough to have a research lab is too large to listen to it.
— *Alan Kay*

◆ Only the ephemeral is of lasting value.
— *Ionesco*

◆ We can't leave the haphazard to chance.
— *N.F. Simpson*

◆ The notes I handle no better than many pianists. But the pauses between notes, ah, is where the art resides.
— *Arthur Schnabel*

◆ A physicist is an atom's way of knowing about atoms.
— *George Wald*

◆ Whenever I'm accosted by panhandlers, I give them a little printed card that says, "I'm sorry, but I spent all of my spare change having these cards printed."
— *Robert Wieder*

◆ There are two kinds of truth, small truth and great truth. You can recognize a small truth because its opposite is a falsehood. The opposite of a great truth is another great truth.
— *Niels Bohr*

◆ Art is a lie that makes us realize the truth.
— *Pablo Picasso*

Consult An Oracle

Many cultures have developed tools that take advantage of our ability to make sense out of ambiguous situations. These tools are called oracles. Some examples include: the ancient Chinese *I Ching*, the Egyptian Tarot, the Nordic Runes, the North American Indian Medicine Wheel, and the Creative Whack Pack. Traditionally, the purpose of using these oracles was not so much to foretell the future, as it was to enable the user to delve deeper into his own intuition when dealing with a problem.

Probably the most famous source of ambiguous pronouncements was the oracle at Delphi in the ancient world. One of the oracle's best known prophecies came in the year 480 B.C. The Persians under Xerxes had invaded the Greek mainland and had successfully conquered two-thirds of the country. Naturally, the Athenian city-fathers were concerned as to which course of action they should take against the oncoming Persians. They re-alized, however, that before any decision could be made, they should send some suppliants to Delphi to get a reading from the oracle. The suppliants made the journey and received the following prophecy:

The wooden wall will save you and your children.

The suppliants took these words back to Athens. At first, the city-fathers were unsure what the prophecy meant. Then one person suggested that they should build a wooden wall up on the Acropolis and take a defensive stand behind it. That's what the "wooden wall" meant — a barricade on the Acropolis.

But the city-fathers knew that the oracle was intentionally ambiguous to force them to go beyond the first right answer. They tried to think of all of the contexts — both literal and metaphorical — in which the words "the wooden wall will save you and your children" would make some sense. After some thought, they came up with another idea. Could the "wooden wall" to which the oracle was referring be the result of all of

the Athenian wooden-hulled ships lined up next to one another? From a distance, the ships would indeed look like a wooden wall. The city-fathers decided, therefore, that the battle should be a naval one rather than a land one.

In 479 B.C., the Athenians went on to rout the Persians in the Battle of Salamis. The oracle's ambiguity forced the Athenians to consult the deeper wisdom of their own intuition, and consider alternatives.

What do you do if you want to tap into your intuition but can't get to Delphi? Why not create your own oracle. It's really quite simple. The following story gives the basic principles at work.

There once was an Indian medicine man whose responsibilities included creating hunting maps for his tribe. Whenever game got sparse, he'd lay a piece of fresh leather out in the sun to dry. Then he'd fold and twist it in his hands, say a few prayers over it, and smooth it out. The rawhide was now crisscrossed with lines and wrinkles. The medicine man marked some basic reference points on the rawhide, and — presto! — a new game map was created. The wrinkles represented new trails the hunters should follow. When the hunters followed the map's newly defined trails, they invariably discovered abundant game.

Moral: By allowing the rawhide's random folds to represent hunting trails, he pointed the hunters to places they previously had not looked.

You can create an oracle in the same way the medicine man did. You'll need three things:

1. A question that you address to the oracle. (The medicine man asked: "Where can more game be found?") This question focuses your thinking.

2. A way to generate a random piece of information. (The medicine man twisted and folded a piece of leather.) The random selection is important. Since people tend to use the same problem-solving approaches repeatedly, they

come up with the same answers. Since a random piece of information is unpredictable, it forces you to look at the problem in a new way.

3. An attitude that interprets the resulting random piece of information as the answer to your question. (The medicine man interpreted the lines as representing new hunting trails.)

You can see that if you have a question and an open, receptive mind, then you're two-thirds of the way toward creating an oracle. Let's run through it step by step.

1. Let's suppose that you're working on a project and wonder, "What should I be thinking about? What should I do next? What's an alternative approach? What aren't I seeing?" First off, clear your mind. Take time to relax and focus your thinking. Now form your question.

2. Now, open your mind up to things that have nothing to do with the idea you're developing. Select something from the world at random. Indeed, constructing the means to get a piece of unexpected information can be both a great way to use your imagination and a lot of fun. It could be one of the following:

◆ Pick out the sixth word on page 247 of your dictionary: *A doorknob.*

◆ Open a magazine. Count the 12th full page advertisement from the front. What product is shown? *A fountain pen.*

◆ Look out the window and find the second thing that has yellow in it: *A tennis ball.*

◆ Open a catalog at random. What's in the upper left hand corner? *Coffee cups.*

◆ Open up the stock section of your newspaper. Go to the third column. Count down to the 16th company whose shares increased in value the previous day. What is their main product? *Water faucets.*

◆ It could be a word that you pick at random on the next page.

maze anvil bait balloon nail key organ skin zone pump parachute program quilt rag powder harbor vertebra glue hair raft lode ruler kitchen robot valley plate mountain needle violin pacemaker soap pen knife piano planet pocket dung powder pump radar halo rubber saddle cup school ship road ball zoo trigger cloud chord chain cannon caldron man woman crystal channel copy cycle plow egg hook drain drum tree bomb wing furniture fungus fork fog flood guitar flag treasure water well girdle glue hair template mirror camera wedge wave sandpaper chessboard desert crown clock cinema food cave staircase network bridge water dust eraser statue net gate pump broom bottleneck ratchet-wheel glacier funhouse fossil block food flower floor antenna god guillotine bee plug blanket funnel book brain brakes booby-trap cesspool cell cancer weed buffer toilet television spring tub compass circle code web dress current detour ear button face factory fairy fan farm feather fertilizer field finger engine floodlight sandwich treasure cup umbrella farm feather fertilizer spectrum template forge adult dope color hole bottle bird trap foot fly foam game garden gear ghost glass graph gun gutter bruise bug circus hammer head heart family blister acid candy chorus springboard fire film festival fence fish eye drill body die spotlight frame glove hand song grave lever sphere square sun table tool trail vent vegetable soup spiral shaft market torpedo thermometer ticket vacuum triangle train torch sword weirdness telescope target spear sponge stomach memory spectrum telephone tapestry kaleidoscope car stove skeleton room treadmill oven filter root temple window star typewriter seed bed fountain armor battery molecule purse library fruit water air earth money spice bell rock album robot farm weapon bank tide bag computer army diamond altar tunnel amoeba anvil bait bible hinge image junk knot sex match manual liquid leg lamp algebra alphabet menu prison monster nest nut opium page parasite pendulum microscope radio puzzle prism port ring pod satellite pill pepper rainbow rudder safe sauce saloon shadow shovel smoke rash horizon mattress map machine lock lever landslide ladder index key ice meteor mist moon music net ocean sphere paint passport perfume river rope pipe plant pond pore prison pyramid record rope rug sand saw screw shell signature herb hose icon horoscope star meat march magnet lode vise nail meter missile motor organ nose onion palette pebble script shoe siren house lightning bridge network eraser laser lens milk mask medal thunder bomb fungus fog soap kite music prison blister toilet pill lode ramp saddle vulture water dust gear blanket garden song rug hook pen knife fork rash weed scale loom rubber hinge ladle landslide lever lock machine mattress copy umbrella hair template farm crystal fossil wedge wave torch root window battery lever keys sponge stomach memory spectrum telephone tapestry kaleidoscope car stove skeleton room treadmill oven filter root temple window star typewriter seed bed fountain armor gutter bruise bug circus hammer head heart family blister acid candy chorus parachute template mountain needle violin pacemaker soap pen knife piano planet pocket dung powder pump radar halo rubber saddle cup school ship road ball rudder safe sauce saloon shadow shovel smoke lamp leg ocean muscle cycle meteor funnel fork rain loans fly dust oven temple star typewriter weapon machine pendulum path objective pool onion treasure fog camera fungus candy shovel torpedo knife planet life stone shell chapter classroom dump robot farm weapon bank tide bag computer army diamond altar tunnel amoeba valley plate sandwich treasure cup stove skeleton room treadmill oven filter root temple window star typewriter seed bed foam game garden gear ghost glass graph gun gutter bruise bug circus hammer head sea herb gangster partner fascist halo nerd trend computer guerilla copy tomb womb comb broom thumb finger footprint palm lotus blossom fool window carpet luck dictionary parasite trashcan door button smudge pimple horseshoe pen thorn suitcase desktop appliance car oracle crown clock cinema food cave staircase network parachute template mountain needle violin pacemaker soap pen knife piano planet pocket dung meat puzzle tunnel amoeba eyeball ear wedge dung meteor oven powder umbrella magic duality partner game wave fork wristwatch keys blister crystal moon music net ocean sphere watch ear lever lock machine weapon mattress oracle

3. Now think how the random thing applies to your situation. Take as much time as you need. There is a connection between the random thing you select and your problem — and your job is to find it. As stated earlier, we humans are quite good at finding patterns and meaning in the world around us — even if none was intended. Thus, whatever you find will have a way of adding insight into your problem and providing clarification.

What are different ways in which it relates to or could apply to your question? Be creative. Go beyond your first answer; look for a second and a third and a fifth right answer. Be literal in your interpretation. Be metaphorical. Be off-the-wall. Be serious.

Think of each random thing as a stimulant to your imagination. Let it spark a series of fresh associations in your mind. Like pebbles dropping in a pond, they will stimulate other associations, some of which may help you find or think of something new. Don't worry how practical or logical you are. What's important is where each random thing leads you.

Most will trigger an immediate response. Sometimes, however, you'll look at one and think, "This doesn't have anything to do with my problem," and be tempted to reject it and reach for a new one. Don't do it. Force yourself to make a connection. Believe that one way or another everything — whether it's cow's milk or anti-war riots, church services or dried flowers, soap bubbles or knight's armor — is connected to everything else.

Remember: Often those ideas that initially seem the least relevant become the most important ones of all because they point to something that you've been completely overlooking.

For example, if "doorknobs" or "water faucets" aren't the typical things you think of when dealing with a problem, then your responses to these ideas are likely to give you new insight into your question.

When should you consult your oracle for another random idea? When you've finished the current one. It might be right now, or it might be next week.

A True-Life Example. Owen Dennis is a resident of Christchurch, New Zealand. Several years ago, it was his job to promote the annual parish fair for his church. He wanted to do something different, something that would really get people's attention. He thought and thought, but nothing amazing came to him. Finally, he decided to pose the problem to an oracle. The problem: "How can I promote my church fund-raiser." The oracle he chose was this book (the very one you're holding in your hands). He said I'll flip this book open at random. The picture on that page will be the answer to my question. The picture he got was on page 38 of the two workmen climbing up the ladders for the Soft and Hard Association Quiz. He thought to himself, "That's my answer!" Now he had to figure out what it meant. He finally got a picture in his mind of the Vicar of his church climbing a ladder up to the bell tower of St. Anne's (13 meters above the ground). He then got the idea that the Vicar, Reverend Simon Ballantyne, would spend forty-eight hours in the bell tower — "a step nearer heaven." Owen talked the Vicar into the stunt. He further promoted it by comparing it to a feat performed by the fourth century ascetic Simeon Stylites, who preached from the top of a pole for thirty-one years. Accompanied by several "good books" and a ham radio, the Vicar survived the stunt in good spirits. His promotion helped the fair raise over $6,000.

Let a random piece
of information
stimulate your thinking.

Listen to Your Dreams

Your dreams are another profound source of ambiguity. How many mornings have you awakened and thought, "What in the world was that dream all about? Why did I dream of catching bugs with a toothbrush? What did it mean that I shot my boss or someone kidnapped my child?" But if you take time to write the dream down and interpret it, you may discover something interesting that will lead your thinking in a whole new direction.

Exercise: Remember a dream you've had recently (or tonight, tell yourself to remember your dream and write it down immediately upon awakening). Now ask yourself these questions:

◆ How do you feel in the dream? (Afraid, strong, vulnerable, in love, crazy, alienated, confident.)

◆ How do you feel about the dream? (Relieved, embarrassed, excited, confused, surprised.)

◆ Who is in the dream? (An old lover, Kermit the Frog, a teacher, a movie star, the Emperor of Japan.)

◆ Where does it take place? (At home, in Russia, in your elementary school, on the planet Jupiter.)

◆ How do the different people react? (Do they run, act silly, or discover a cure for cancer?)

Now interpret these self-generated picture stories. Think of them as symbols through which your unconscious mind is speaking to you. Think of them as you would an oracle. Go beyond your first right answer and look for a second and a third. If you dream someone kidnaps your children, you might take it as a sign that you should spend more time with them. It might also mean that you believe someone is stealing your ideas. Or perhaps it means that you've been too serious (your childlike side has been abducted) and you should be more playful.

If you dream of death, it doesn't necessarily mean the person has died, but that what they represent to you has changed. Pregnancy could signify a new idea you're conceiving. You may dream of school and all that entails: losing your homework, being late for class, or missing a test. This may reflect a new situation in which you feel like a student again, and parts of your performance are inadequate or out of control.

Your dream may lead you to a new furniture design, a different way of dealing with your manager, or you may get an insight into a problem. You may also get a fresh insight into yourself. My daughter dreamed that giants were chasing her. The only escape was through a small square hole in a door. Her grandmother said, "No, we can't make it," but Athena said, "Yes, we can if we wiggle like this," and they escaped. She woke up feeling good about herself knowing that her ingenuity and persistence had helped her solve a problem. My wife has had a series of dreams of being in a theater. During the course of ten years she has moved from being in the audience, to part of the chorus, to serving as an understudy, to being the star, to writing her own script.

Remember: your dreams are uniquely yours. Take advantage of them to help you resolve conflicts, inspire solutions, and suggest new approaches. How can you relate a recent dream to a current problem?

Summary

Most of us have learned to "avoid ambiguity" because of the communication problems it can cause. This is an especially good idea in practical situations where the consequences of such a misunderstanding would be serious. For example, a fire chief fighting a three-alarm fire needs to issue his orders with utmost clarity so as to leave nothing to question.

In imaginative situations, however, there is the danger that too much specificity can stifle your imagination. Let's suppose that the same fire chief has asked you to paint a mural on the side of his firehouse. If he tells you what he wants it to look like right down to the last detail, he hasn't given you any room for your imagination. Perhaps, if the assignment were stated somewhat ambiguously, then you would have more room to think and be creative. In other words, there is a place for ambiguity — perhaps not so much when you're evaluating and executing ideas, but certainly when you're searching for and playing with them.

TIP: Take advantage of the ambiguity in the world. Look at something and think about what else it might be.

TIP: If you're giving someone a problem that has the potential of being solved in a creative way, then you might try—at least initially — posing it in an ambiguous fashion so as not to restrict their imagination.

TIP: Let the world be your oracle. Allow random, unexpected information to stimulate your imagination.

TIP: Listen to your dreams.

9. To Err Is Wrong

Hits and Misses

In the summer of 1979, Boston Red Sox first baseman Carl Yastrzemski became the fifteenth player in baseball history to reach the three thousand hit plateau. This event drew a lot of media attention, and for about a week prior to the attainment of this goal, hundreds of reporters covered Yaz's every move. Finally, one reporter asked, "Hey Yaz, aren't you afraid all of this attention will go to your head?" Yastrzemski replied, "I look at it this way: in my career I've been up to bat over ten thousand times. That means I've been unsuccessful at the plate over seven thousand times. That fact alone keeps me from getting a swollen head."

Most people consider success and failure as opposites, but they are actually both products of the same process. As Yaz suggests, an activity that produces a hit may also produce a miss. It's the same with creative thinking. The same energy that generates creative ideas also produces errors.

Many people are not comfortable with errors. Our educational system, based on the "right answer" belief, cultivates our thinking in another, more conservative way. From an early age, we are taught that right answers are good and incorrect answers are bad. This value is deeply embedded in the incentive system used in most schools:

Right over 90% of the time = "A"

Right over 80% of the time = "B"

Right over 70% of the time = "C"

Right over 60% of the time = "D"

Less than 60% correct, you fail

From this we learn to be right as often as possible and to keep our mistakes to a minimum. We learn, in other words, that "to err is wrong."

With this attitude, you won't be taking many chances. If you learn that failing even a little penalizes you (e.g., being wrong only 15% of the time garners you only a "B" performance), you learn not to make mistakes. And more important, you learn not to put yourself in situations where you might fail. This leads to conservative thought patterns designed to avoid "failure."

I have a friend who graduated from college with a master's degree in journalism. For six months, she tried to find a job, but to no avail. I talked with her about her situation, and realized that her problem was that she didn't know how to fail. She went through eighteen years of schooling without ever failing an examination, a paper, a midterm, a pop-quiz, or a final. So she was reluctant to try any approaches where she might fail. She had been conditioned to believe that failure is bad in and of itself, rather than a stepping stone to new ideas. Look around. How many people do you see who are afraid to try something new because of this fear of failure? Most of us have learned not to make mistakes in public. As a result, we remove ourselves from many learning experiences except for those occurring in the most private of circumstances.

A Different Logic

A man's errors are his portals of discovery.

— James Joyce, Author

From a practical standpoint, "to err is wrong" makes sense. Our survival in the everyday world requires us to perform thousands of small tasks without much thought. Think about it: you wouldn't last very long if you were to step out in front of traffic or stick your hand into a pot of boiling water. In addition, engineers whose bridges collapse, stock brokers who lose money for their clients, and copywriters whose ad campaigns decrease sales won't keep their jobs very long.

Nevertheless, too great an adherence to the belief "to err is wrong" can greatly undermine your attempts to generate new ideas. If you're more concerned with producing right answers than generating original ideas, you'll probably make uncritical use of the rules, formulae, and procedures used to obtain these right answers. By doing this, you'll bypass the imaginative phase of the creative process, and thus spend little time testing assumptions, challenging the rules, asking what if, or just plain fooling around with the problem. All of these techniques will produce some incorrect answers, but in the imaginative phase errors are a necessary by-product of creative thinking. As Yaz would put it, "If you want the hits, be prepared for the misses." That's the way the game of life goes.

Whenever an error pops us, the usual response is "Jeez, another screwup, what went wrong this time?" The creative thinker, on the other hand, will realize the potential value of errors, and perhaps say something like, "Would you look at that! Where can it lead our thinking?" And then he or she will go on to use the error as a stepping stone to a new idea. As a matter of fact, the whole history of discovery is filled with people who used erroneous assumptions and failed ideas as stepping stones to new ideas. Columbus thought he was finding a shorter route to India. Johannes Kepler stumbled on to the idea of interplanetary gravity because of assumptions which were right for the wrong reasons. Thomas Edison knew 1,800 ways *not* to build a light bulb. Freud had several big failures before he developed psychoanalysis. One of Madame Curie's failures was radium.

Automotive inventor Charles Kettering, one of the 20th century's great creative minds, had this to say about the value of learning to fail:

> An inventor is simply a person who doesn't take his education too seriously. You see, from the time a person is six years old until he graduates from college he has to take three or four examinations a year. If he flunks once, he is out. But an inventor is almost always failing. He tries and fails maybe a thousand times. If he succeeds once then he's in. These two things are diametrically opposite. We often say that the biggest job we have is to teach a newly hired employee how to fail intelligently. We have to train him to experiment over and over and to keep on trying and failing until he learns what will work.

Nature serves as a good example of how trial and error can be used to make changes. Every now and then genetic mutations occur — errors in gene reproduction. Most of the time, these mutations have a deleterious effect on the species, and they drop out of the gene pool. But occasionally, a mutation provides the species with something beneficial, and that change will be passed on to future generations. The rich variety of all species is due to this trial and error process. If there had never been any mutations from the first amoeba, where would we be now?

Is Failure Bad?

If you hit every time, the target is too near or too big.

—Tom Hirshfield, Physicist

Your error rate in any activity is a function of your familiarity with that activity. If you are doing things that are routine for you, then you will probably make very few errors. But if you are doing things that have no precedence in your experience or are trying different approaches, then you will be making your share of mistakes. Innovators may not bat a thousand — far from it — but they do get new ideas.

Errors serve a useful purpose: they tell us when to change direction. When things go smoothly, we generally don't think about them. To a great extent, this is because we function according to the principle of negative feedback. Often it is only when things or people fail to do their job that they get our attention. For example, you are probably not thinking about your kneecaps right now. That's because everything is fine with them. The same goes for your elbows: they are also performing their function — no problem at all. But if you were to break a leg, you would immediately notice all the things you could no longer do, but which you used to take for granted.

Negative feedback means that the current approach is not working, and it is up to you to find a new one. We learn by trial and error, not by trial and rightness. If we did things correctly every time, we would never have to change course, and we'd end up with more of the same.

After the supertanker *Exxon Valdez* broke open off of Alaska in the spring of 1989, thereby polluting the coast with millions of gallons of oil, the oil industry was forced to rethink and toughen up many of its safety standards regarding petroleum transport. The same thing happened after the accident at the

Three Mile Island nuclear reactor in 1979 — many safety standards were changed. The explosion of the *Challenger* space shuttle caused a similar thing to happen. Similarly, the sinking of the *Titanic* led to the creation of the International Ice Patrol, and legally mandated iceberg reporting.

I like to ask people if they've ever been fired from a job. If they have, they typically say something along the lines of "Yeah, it was really traumatic, but it turned out to be the best thing that ever happened to me. It forced me to come to grips with who I was as a person. I had to look at my strengths and weaknesses with no delusions at all. It forced me to get out of my box and scramble. Six months later, I was in a much better situation."

We learn by our failures. A person's errors are the whacks that lead him or her to think something different.

Is Success Good?

This leads to another question: Is success a good thing? Sometimes the answer isn't so obvious. Just as it's possible that failure can lead to something good, sometimes success can lead to something bad. There are two ways in which this can happen.

First, success tends to lock you in a pattern, and you get the attitude, "If it's not broken, why fix it?" This attitude prevents you from experimenting and trying other approaches that in the long run may do you a lot more good.

Second, success — perversely enough — can create situations that undermine your original intentions and end up creating bigger problems than the ones you started with.

Here are some examples:

◆ In preparing for the Olympics, the coach of a leading crew team invited a meditation instructor to teach awareness techniques to his crew. He hoped that such training would enhance their rowing effectiveness and improve their sense of unity. As the crew learned more about meditation, they became more synchronized, their strokes got smoother, and there was less resistance. The irony is that their performance decreased and they went slower. It turned out that the crew was more interested in being in harmony than in winning. So the meditation teacher was dismissed.

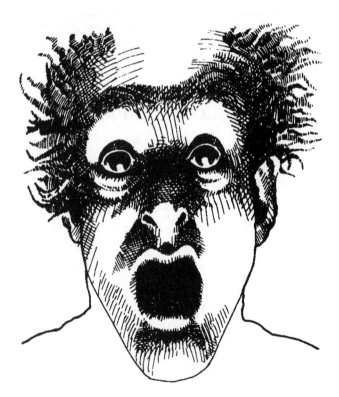

◆ During the Soviet-Afghanistan war, the Soviets believed that their savage attacks on the civilian population would intimidate the Afghans into submission. Ironically, their attacks had just the opposite result. Because Afghan warriors historically stayed close to home to guard their women and children, the Soviets' driving Afghan dependents into refugee camps liberated the Mujahideen from family responsibilities and turned them into formidable opponents.

◆ France's mobilization efforts in the first weeks of World War II were so successful that tens of thousands of key workers in vital war industries enlisted. As a result, these industries were practically brought to a halt, thereby placing the country at even greater risk. Several months later, the new recruits were returned to their jobs.

◆ In the mid-1960's, the Japanese resort town of Atami lobbied hard to get a high-speed "bullet train" link to Tokyo, then three hours away. After the railway was completed, tourism declined — in part because the romance of going away for the weekend was lost in a place that could be reached in only fifty minutes.

Is success good? Is failure bad? Well, like Yaz, I'd rather have a higher batting average than a lower one. Nonetheless, as I look back over my life, I find that I was successful at some endeavors where I would have been better off had I failed. That's because the success prevented me from experimenting and trying different approaches. Conversely, there are places where I'm glad I failed because it forced me to look for a second right answer that, in hindsight, was much preferable to the first.

Summary

There are places where errors are inappropriate, but the imaginative phase of the creative process isn't one of them. Errors are a sign that you are diverging from the well-traveled path. A large part of creative thinking is not being afraid to fail. As director Woody Allen put it, "If you're not failing every now and again, it's a sign you're not trying anything very innovative."

Remember these two benefits of failure. First, if you do fail, you learn what doesn't work. Second, the failure gives you an opportunity to try a new approach.

TIP: If you make an error, use it as a stepping stone to an idea you might not otherwise have discovered.

TIP: Differentiate between errors of "commission" and those of "omission." The latter can be more costly than the former. If you're not making many errors, you might ask yourself, "How many opportunities am I missing by not being more aggressive."

TIP: Before embarking on an idea or project, ask yourself: "What bad things can happen if we're successful?"

10. I'm Not Creative

Self-Fulfilling Prophecies

What concerns me is not the way things are, but rather the way people think things are.

— Epictetus, Philosopher

Some years ago, Johnny Carson made a joke on his television show that there was a toilet paper shortage in this country. He then went on to describe what some of the consequences of this shortage might be. The implication of this joke was that the viewers had better go out and stock up on toilet paper right away or else they would have to face these consequences. The subject made for a good laugh, since there was, in fact, no toilet paper shortage at all. Within days, however, a real shortage did develop. Because people thought there was a shortage, they bought up all of the toilet paper they could find, and, as a result, they disrupted the normal flow of toilet paper distribution.

This serves as a good example of the self-fulfilling prophecy. This is the phenomenon whereby a person believes something to be true (which may or may not be so), acts on that belief, and by his actions causes the belief to become true. As you can see, the self-fulfilling prophecy is a case where the world of thought overlaps with the world of action. And it happens in all avenues of life.

Business people are quite familiar with self-fulfilling prophecies. In fact, the whole notion of business confidence is based on them. If a person thinks that the market is healthy (even though it may not be), he will invest money in it. This raises other people's confidence, and pretty soon the market will be healthy.

Educators are also aware of self-fulfilling prophecies. A few years ago, a teacher in New York was told that she had a class of gifted children, when in fact she had an ordinary class. As a result, she went out of her way to develop her students. She spent more time preparing her lessons and staying after class to give them ideas. The class, in turn, responded in a positive way and scored higher than average on the same tests that had previously classified them as mediocre. Because they were treated as gifted children, they performed as gifted children.

This also happens in sales. Several years ago, I did a seminar with the direct sales force of a large pharmaceutical company. Prior to the session, I had an opportunity to talk to the people in the bottom 25% of sales performance. I asked them, "Why aren't you more successful?" They answered with such comments as:

> **"Our products cost too much."**
> **"I've got a crummy territory."**
> **"I don't get along with my manager."**
> **"The moon is in Sagittarius."**

What was their problem? They weren't taking responsibility for their own performance. They spent their time creating excuses rather than innovative sales solutions.

I then talked to the top sales performers. These people were happy, having fun, and achieving their goals. I asked them what the key to their success was. They said such things as:

> When I look at myself in the mirror in the morning, I see the face of a person who is going to accomplish wonderful things. If I get turned down by a physician or a nurse, I think of a second way to get the business, a third way, and sometimes even a fifth way. I'm going to out-think the competition. I'm going to out-hustle the competition. And that's the way it works out. It's a self-fulfilling prophecy.

The same phenomenon is also found in athletics. I've noticed that one of the chief differences between winners and losers is that winners see themselves as winning and losers generally give themselves a reason or an excuse to lose. A person who exemplifies this is Bob Hopper, a college teammate of mine. Bob was a champion swimmer who rarely lost a race. One day at the pool, I asked him why he was so successful at competitive swimming. He responded:

> There are several reasons. First, my strokes are all well-developed. Second, I work out hard. Third, I take good care of myself and eat right. But my top competitors also do these things. So the key difference between just "being good" and "winning" is my mental preparation before each meet.
>
> Starting each day before the meet, I run the following movie through my mind. I see myself coming into the Natatorium, with three thousand cheering fans in the stands. I see the lights reflecting off the water. I see myself going up to the starting blocks. I see my competitors on each side. I hear the gun go off, and see myself diving into the pool and taking the first stroke of butterfly. I feel myself pulling through, then taking another stroke, and then another. I see myself coming to the wall, turning, and pushing off into the backstroke with a small lead. The lead gets bigger as I kick hard. Then I push off into the breaststroke. That's my best stroke and that's where I really open it up. Then I bring it home in the freestyle. I see myself winning! I run this movie through my mind thirty or forty times before each meet. When it comes time to swim, I just get in and win.

All of these examples show that just thinking a particular thought can have an enormous impact on the world of action.

Give Yourself A Creative License

Exercise: Are you creative? (Check the appropriate box.)

☐ Yes   ☐ No

Several years ago, a major oil company was concerned about the lack of creative productivity among its engineers. To deal with this problem, a team of psychologists was brought in to find out what differentiated the creative people from the less creative ones. They hoped that their findings could be used to stimulate the less creative people.

The psychologists asked the engineers many, many questions ranging from where they grew up to what their educational backgrounds were to what their favorite colors were. After three months of study, the psychologists found that the chief differentiating factor that separated the two groups was:

The creative people thought they were creative, and the less creative people didn't think they were.

As a consequence, the people who didn't think they were creative never put themselves in a position where they could use their creativity. They didn't allow themselves to get into an imaginative frame of mind, play with their knowledge, take a few risks, or look for the seventh right answer.

Some "I'm not creative" people stifle themselves because they think that creativity belongs only to the Einsteins, Curies, and Shakespeares of the world. To be sure, these are some of the superluminaries of the creative firmament, but by and large, these people didn't get their big ideas right out of the blue. On

the contrary, most of their big ideas came from paying attention to their medium-size ideas, playing with them, and turning
them into big ideas. The same thing holds for most medium-
size ideas. These come from small ideas which their creators
paid attention to, and gradually worked into bigger things.

Thus, one of the major factors that differentiates creative
people from less creative people is that creative people give
themselves a license to pay attention to their small ideas. Even
though they don't know where one of these will lead, they know
that a small idea could lead to a big breakthrough, and they
believe that they are capable of making it happen.

If you think you're creative, then you'll put yourself in situations where you can use your creativity, take a few risks, try
some new approaches, and come up with new ideas.

Summary

The worlds of thought and action overlap. What you think
has a way of becoming true. If you want to be more creative,
believe in the worth of your ideas, and have the persistence to
continue building on them. With this attitude, you'll take more
risks, and break the rules occasionally. You'll look for more than
one right answer, explore for ideas outside your area, tolerate
ambiguity, be foolish every now and then, play a little bit, en-
gage in asking "what if" questions, and be motivated to go beyond the status quo. And finally, you'll be able to whack yourself into doing all of these things.

A Whack on the Other Side of the Head

The Student Returns to the Creativity Teacher

Some people have ideas. A few carry them into the world of action and make them happen. These are the innovators.

— Andrew Mercer, Innovator

A few months after his initial encounter with the creativity teacher, the student returned to tell him of his progress. "Things are really cooking," he said enthusiastically. "I've opened up my mental locks, and I'm getting all kinds of ideas. I take time to ask 'what if' and explore in outside areas. I used to loathe problems, but now when they pop up, my mind dances looking for opportunities. When I evaluate ideas, I try to use even the stupidest ones as stepping stones to something new."

The teacher replied, "What are you going to do with these new ideas?"

"I haven't really decided. But I'm getting ready to do something," he answered.

At this point, the teacher picked up a stick and gave him a whack on the *other* side of the head. The student was stunned. The teacher followed that act with this counsel: "Ideas are great, but they aren't worth much if you don't use them. It's important for you to get your ideas into action. Your problem is that you're not using all four roles of the creative process."

The student replied, "The four roles of the creative process? What are they?"

"Listen carefully, and I'll give you an in-depth explanation," said the creativity teacher. "Over the years, I've had an opportunity to work with many creative people: software developers, television producers, students, comedians, journalists, coaches, scientists, and designers. Again and again, I've noticed a common pattern in how they generate, manage, and apply new ideas.

"The hallmark of creative people is their mental flexibility. They are able to shift in and out of different types of thinking depending on the needs of the situation at hand. Sometimes, they're open and probing, at others, they're playful and off-the-wall. At still others, they're critical and fault-finding. And finally, they're doggedly persistent in striving to reach their goals. From this, I've concluded that people who are successful in the creative process are able to adopt four main roles, each of which embodies a different type of thinking. These roles are:

Explorer

Artist

Judge

Warrior

"Let's take a closer look," said the creativity teacher.

"First off, you — as a creative thinker — need the raw materials from which new ideas are made: facts, concepts, experiences, knowledge, feelings, and whatever else you can find. However, you're much more likely to find something original if you venture off the beaten path. So, you become an **Explorer** and look for the materials you'll use to build your idea. During the course of your searching, you'll poke around in unknown areas, pay attention to unusual patterns, use different senses, and seek out a variety of different information.

"For the most part, the ideas and information you gather as an explorer will be like so many pieces of colored glass at the end of a kaleidoscope. They may form a pattern, but if you want something new and different, you'll have to give them a twist or two. That's when you shift roles and let the **Artist** in you come out. You experiment with a variety of approaches. You follow your intuition. You rearrange things, look at things backwards, and turn them upside down. You ask 'what if' questions and look for hidden analogies. You may even break the rules or create your own. After all of this you come up with a new idea.

"Now, you ask yourself, 'Is this idea any good? Is it worth pursuing? Will it give me the return I want? Do I have the resources to make it happen?' To help you make your decision, you adopt the mindset of a **Judge**. During your evaluation, you critically weigh the evidence. You look for drawbacks in the idea, and wonder if the timing is right. You run risk analyses, question your assumptions, and listen to your gut. Ultimately you make a decision.

"Finally it's time to implement your idea. You realize, however, that the world isn't set up to accommodate every new idea
that comes along. As a matter of fact, there's a lot of competition out there. If you want your idea to succeed, you'll have to
take the offensive. So, you become a **Warrior** and take your idea
into action. As a warrior, you're part general and part foot-sol-
dier. You develop your strategy, and commit yourself to reaching your objective. You also have to have the discipline to slog
it out in the trenches. You may have to overcome excuses, idea
killers, temporary setbacks, and other obstacles. But you have
the courage to do what's necessary to make your idea a reality.

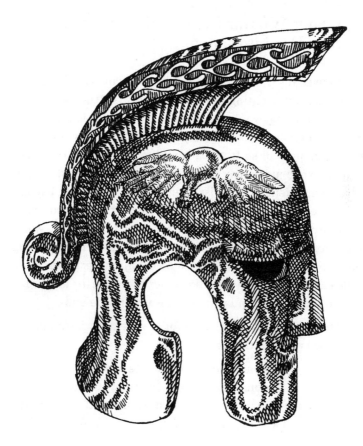

"To summarize:

♦ Your Explorer is your role for searching for new information and resources;

♦ Your Artist is your role for turning these resources into new ideas;

♦ Your Judge is your role for evaluating the merits of an idea and deciding what to do with it; and,

♦ Your Warrior is your role for carrying your idea into action.

"Viewed together, these four roles are your team for generating and implementing new ideas. Of course, the pattern for most of the things you create won't always be this linear progression of explorer-to-artist-to-judge-to-warrior. Usually there is a fair amount of shifting back and forth between roles. For example, your judge may return an idea to your artist for further development. Your artist might come up with an idea and tell your explorer to go dig up some information that supports it. Your warrior will tell your judge what's making it in the world and what's not — thus sharpening the latter's decision-making ability. In general, however, you'll be using your explorer more in the early stages of the creative process, your artist and judge more in the middle, and your warrior toward the end.

"There are two main reasons for low creative performance: weak roles and bad timing.

"Imagine the consequences of having a weak role in your creative team. If your explorer has his head in the sand, you won't have any new information to draw upon. If your artist's imagination is locked up, you'll end up with run-of-the-mill ideas that lack a punch. If your judge's critical faculties are out-to-lunch, then you may be saying 'yes' to garbage and 'no' to potentially good ideas. And if you've got a wimp for a warrior, then you won't be getting many ideas into action. Thus, you have to make a deliberate effort to get and keep all your creative roles in good shape. The maxim use it or lose it applies as much to creative thinking as it does to any other activity.

"Equally important to knowing your creative roles is knowing *when to use them* — timing is paramount. Using a role at the wrong time — such as employing your judge to explore for information or your artist to implement your idea — is counterproductive. It's like driving on the freeway in reverse or trying to back into a parking place in fourth gear. When your timing's off, you won't get much accomplished. Thus, you need to pay attention to the type of thinking required for each situation and then shift into it.

"Some people have trouble shifting because they get stuck in a particular role. This can have disastrous results on their creative performance. For example, if you get stuck in your explorer, you may never get around to assembling the information you've gathered into a new idea. If you get stuck in your artist, you may spend all of your time working and re-working your creation and not let go of it. If you get stuck in your judge, you'll inhibit your artist and spend so long evaluating your idea that you'll fail to make a timely decision. And, if you get stuck in your warrior, you'll want to rush everything into action whether the other roles have done their job or not.

"Thus, my prescription for high performance is to develop your creative roles and make sure you use them at the appropriate time."

The student listened to all of this and said, "What you say makes a lot of sense. Let's apply it to my situation."

"All right," replied the creativity teacher. "How adventurous and perceptive is your explorer?"

"I'm looking for ideas in a lot of different places. I'm looking for the second and third right answers. I'm more tolerant of ambiguity."

"How about your artist?"

"Highly imaginative. I'm asking 'what if,' challenging the rules, and looking at things in different ways."

"And your judge?"

"I've become more discerning. I'm critical, but I'm also constructive — I use even the stupidest ideas as stepping stones to practical, creative ideas. I also try to go after my sacred cows. I even sometimes allow myself to play the fool to knock myself out of group-think situations."

"And your warrior."

"Well, I've got a bunch of ideas and I'm thinking about using them."

"There's your problem: you're just generating ideas. You need to activate your warrior and get your ideas into action. Here are some tips to help you do this."

Take A Whack At It

You can't hit a home run unless you step up to the plate. You can't catch fish unless you put your line in the water. You can't make your idea a reality unless you take a whack at it. Many of our personal goals are stranded on a little island called the "Someday I'll." Don't wait for your idea to happen. Make it happen. As adman Carl Ally put it, "Either you let your life slip away by not doing the things you want to do, or you get up and do them." If you want to be a singer, go sing. Sing in the shower. Sing for your friends. Join the choir. Audition for a musical. Start now. **What are three things you can do to reach your goal?**

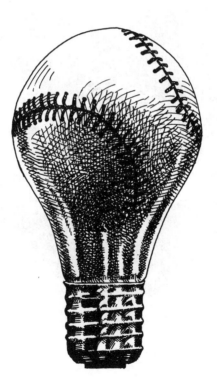

Put A Lion in Your Heart

"To fight a bull when you're not scared is nothing," says a well-known bull fighter. "And not to fight a bull when you are scared is nothing. But to fight a bull when you are scared — that is something." What gives you the courage to act on your ideas? Having a well-thought-out plan? Encouragement? Faith in the idea? Past success? **What puts a lion in your heart?**

Get Support

One reason gypsies have a good health record is the role the family plays in establishing a positive health environment. When a gypsy gets sick, it's not uncommon for six or eight other gypsies to accompany her to the doctor. Such family participation provides not only a support system for the ill member, it also creates a high expectancy for getting well. Similarly, it's much easier to be creative if your environment both supports and *expects* new ideas. **How can you create a support system around you?**

Get Rid of Excuses

When the Spanish explorer Cortez landed at Veracruz, the first thing he did was burn his ships. Then he told his men: "You can either fight or die." Burning his ships removed a third alternative: giving up and returning to Spain. Sometimes it takes more creativity to get rid of the excuses we put in the way than it does to come up with the idea in the first place. **What three factors will make it difficult for you to reach your objective? How can you get rid of these excuses?**

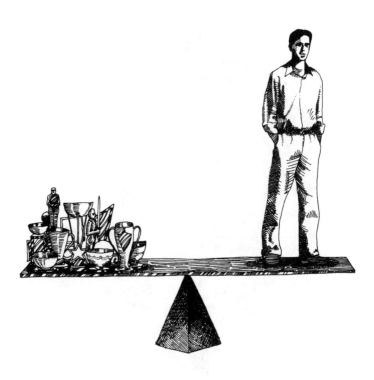

Slay A Dragon

Long ago, mapmakers sketched dragons on maps as a sign to sailors that they would be entering unknown territory at their own risk. Some sailors took this sign literally and were afraid to venture on. Others saw the dragons as a sign of opportunity, a door to virgin territory. Similarly, each of us has a mental map of the world complete with dragons. **Where does fear hold you back? What dragons can you slay?**

Flex Your Risk Muscle

Strengthen your "risk muscle." Everyone has one. You keep it in shape by trying new things. If you don't, it atrophies and you're no longer able to take chances. Make it a point to take at least one risk every week. How can you exercise your risk muscle today? Try a new recipe. Invest in a new idea. Tackle a problem outside your field of expertise. As Arthur Koestler put it: "If the Creator had a purpose in equipping us with a neck, he certainly would have meant for us to stick it out." **How can you flex your risk muscle?**

Have Something At Stake

A frozen-fish processor had trouble selling a new line of frozen fish because it tasted "flat." The company tried everything to keep the fish fresh including holding them in tanks until just before processing — but to no avail. Then someone suggested: "Put a predator in there with them — that should keep them fresh." This idea worked like a charm. The fish kept moving and retained their vitality. Moral: have something at stake — survival, self-esteem, money, reputation — so that you'll be motivated to make your idea successful. **What do you have at stake?**

Be Dissatisfied

An inventor was asked why he spent sixteen hours every day tinkering with his work. "Because I'm dissatisfied with everything as it currently exists in its present form." Dissatisfaction can be beneficial to the creative process. Otherwise you lose the prod you need to spot potential problems and opportunities. **What are you dissatisfied about? How can you turn irritation into inspiration?**

Use Your Shield

"The only person who likes change is a wet baby," observes educator Roy Blitzer. Two basic rules of life are: 1) change is inevitable; and 2) everybody resists change. New ideas can be threatening, and they often provoke a negative reaction. For example, when Stravinsky first presented his *Rite of Spring* ballet with its unusual harmonies and primitive rhythms, he was met with a rioting audience. When Kepler correctly solved the orbital problem of the planets by using ellipses rather than circles, he was denounced. Be prepared for such a reaction and don't let it prevent you from acting on your idea. As German statesman Konrad Adenauer put it, "A thick skin is a gift from God." **What negative reaction do you expect? How can you deflect it?**

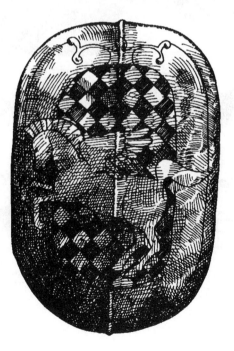

Sell, Sell, Sell

"It's not creative unless it sells," goes the advertising line. You can have the greatest idea in the world, but if you can't sell it, you won't get very far. What are three reasons that someone else would want your idea or product? What benefits does it provide? What does it promise? **How can you make your idea more attractive to other people?**

Set A Deadline

For many people, the ultimate inspiration is the deadline. That's when you have to put away your excuses and get down to the business of making your idea happen. What's your objective? Can you state it in a simple sentence? What are the three key things you'll need to do to reach it? **Where is your sense of urgency? What tight deadlines can you give yourself?**

Be Persistent

Once upon a time, two frogs fell into a bucket of cream. The first frog, seeing that there was no way to get any footing in the white fluid, accepted his fate and drowned.

The second frog didn't like that approach. He started thrashing around in the cream and doing whatever he could to stay afloat. After a while, his churning turned the cream into butter, and he was able to hop out. **How persistent are you?**

The student listened to all of this and said, "Thanks a lot. I appreciate your giving me these additional whacks. Now I'll put my ideas into action."

"You're welcome," said the creativity teacher. "Oh, yes, there's one more piece of advice I can give you."

"What's that?"

"After you implement your idea, give yourself a pat on the back. And then go out and earn another one."

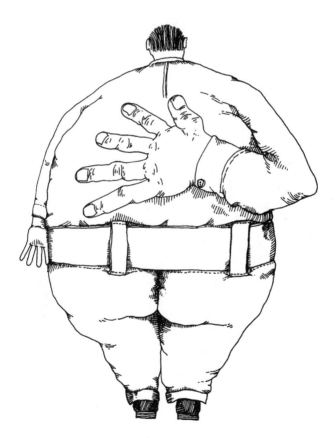

Ancient Whacks
of Heraclitus

I am often asked, "Roger, who inspired you to study creativity? Who got you started trying to look at things in different ways?" They are are quite surprised when I give them the answer. It is Heraclitus of Ephesus, the most provocative and intriguing of the ancient Greek philosophers. I first came in contact with him in the late 1960's when I was studying classical Greek. I've been consulting Heraclitus ever since, and he never ceases to provide me with creative insight. Indeed, if creative thinking involves imagining things in a fresh light, questioning assumptions, and discovering connections among various phenomena, then I believe that Heraclitus is the world's first "creativity teacher." His ideas both inspire us to think in these ways, and also provide us with strategies to understand the world in a fresh manner. In this final chapter, I would like to share with you some of Heraclitus' ideas and also present my interpretations of his work. I believe that Heraclitus is a fitting conclusion to this book because his thought will "whack" your thinking. Indeed, you can think of this chapter as your "final exam."

Heraclitus' epigrams about life, nature, and the cosmos were known throughout the ancient world. And still today, 2,500 years later, his ideas retain their freshness, relevance, and — yes! — their power to stimulate your thinking. So seminal are Heraclitus' ideas that over the past two and a half millennia, some of the world's most profound thinkers have seen in them the seeds of their own beliefs. Among these include: Plato, Aristotle, the Stoics, Bishop Hippolytus, and Plotinus in antiquity; and Goethe, Hegel, Marx, Nietzsche, Jung, and Cassirer in recent centuries.

Even to his contemporaries, Heraclitus was known by such epithets as the "The Enigmatic One" and the "Riddler." And for good reason: his use of metaphor, symbol, and paradox makes him sound more like a poet or religious prophet than a philosopher. Thus, when you consult Heraclitus, you enter a vividly surreal world: he describes his philosophic vision with images of flowing rivers and barking dogs, garbage-loving donkeys, and pain-inflicting doctors, smoke-sensing nostrils and life-giving sea water. But against this backdrop emerges a philosophy of the creative spirit. His message is: "Wake up and pay attention to what's happening around you and within you, and then act on what you've found." As Heraclitus himself put it, "Do not act and speak like those asleep."

Heraclitus' Life and Times

According to ancient sources, Heraclitus "flourished" — that is, was in his forties — around 500 B.C. This dating is significant because it means that he was an almost exact contemporary of the Chinese thinkers Confucius and Lao-Tzu, and also the Indian contemplative Siddartha Gautama (*The Buddha*).

Heraclitus lived in turbulent times. Within his lifetime, long-standing empires suddenly fell, and new ones arose and aggressively pressed for advantage. This reversal of fortune was not lost on him. He says: "War is father of all and king of all. He renders some gods, others men; he makes some slaves, others free."

Not much is known about his life, and most of that is anecdotal. Heraclitus lived in the prosperous Greek Ionian coastal city-state of Ephesus (now western Turkey). Supposedly, he was a member of the Ephesian royal family and in line for the kingship there, but he ceded his title to his brother. It's said that he was contemptuous of his fellow human beings. The ancient biographer Diogenes Laertius tells the story that one day a group of Ephesian citizens found Heraclitus playing dice with some children, and asked him why. He replied: "Why are you surprised, you good-for-nothings? Isn't this better than playing politics with you?"

Heraclitus was present at the dawn of philosophy. He and the other early philosophers — Thales, Pythagoras, Parmenides, and Democritus (this group later known as the "Pre-Socratics" because they laid the conceptual foundations for Socrates and Plato) — were very curious people who asked big questions. Philosophy means "love of wisdom" and that's what they were after: "What is the truth of the cosmos? How do we get knowledge? How should we live?"

To find his answers, Heraclitus created his own approach to understand reality: he paid close attention to what was happening around him, and then thought about it until it made sense to him. Heraclitus felt that consulting one's own intuition was the appropriate method for philosophical investigation. As he put it: "I searched into myself." Diogenes Laertius writes, "He was no man's disciple, but said that he searched himself and learned everything from himself." We can say, moreover, that Heraclitus is the first Western philosopher beginning from a point of view of stated self-consciousness.

It's not known if Heraclitus wrote a book. Perhaps he just put together a collection of his sayings. All that remains of his thought are approximately 125 epigrams (called "fragments" by the 19th century German compiler of his works, Hermann Diels). Interestingly, all of these epigrams have been passed down to us as quotes and inclusions in other writers' works.

Heraclitus was sure of his own vision, disdainful of mediocrity, and scornful of all laziness: intellectual, physical, and moral. This is reflected in his statement: "If happiness consisted in the pleasures of the body, we should call oxen happy whenever they enounter fodder to eat."

Solve the Ancient Whacks

As I mentioned, Heraclitus was known to his contemporaries as the "Enigmatic One." There are several reasons for this. The first is that Heraclitus believed that reality itself is an enigma. As he put it: "Things love to conceal their true nature." But he also believed that this enigma can be understood, and that the key to solving it consists not so much in having more information but rather in finding new and different ways of thinking about the information that we do have. Heraclitus was certain that if you have a creative thinking mindset, then solutions to the problems you deal with will become obvious.

What's intriguing is the manner in which he expresses himself in these epigrams: he wrote in a style that is best described as intentionally enigmatic. This leads to the second reason for Heraclitus' epithet as the "Enigmatic One." Heraclitus felt that the truth is precious, and that people appreciate it more fully if they have to actively participate in finding it. His style — similar to a Zen teacher's paradoxical *koan* or a Delphic Oracle ambiguous prophecy — was designed to "whack" people out of their habitual thought patterns so that they might look at what they are doing in a fresh way.

An important consequence of Heraclitus' enigmatic style is that he not only challenges us to think, he also requires us to change the way we think. It's as though each "Whack" is a creativity exercise that you have to solve in order to get its meaning. To understand him, you have to adopt a frame of mind in which you tolerate ambiguity, view things metaphorically, challenge your assumptions, reverse your expectations, and probe below the surface for hidden meanings. These are all things that have been discussed in this book about how to develop a creative attitude.

This chapter contains thirty Ancient Whacks. They are listed on pages 200-229. Taken as a whole, these wonderful jewels of insight provide us with a set of instructions on how to be more creative. My challenge to you is to figure out what each of them means to you.

I have provided my own interpretations for each Ancient Whack. If you disagree with or dislike these interpretations, so much the better! I encourage you to put on your "creative thinking hat" and come up with your own. That's the beauty of working with Heraclitus: there's no one right answer! Indeed, sometimes I don't agree with myself. If, as Heraclitus put it, "You can't step into the same river twice," then my own state of mind can never be quite the same, and my own interpretations change. And the same will be true for you: the Ancient Whacks will continue to take on new and fresh meanings!

I hope you enjoy and benefit from using Heraclitus' wisdom to spur your creativity!

The source for the original ancient Greek is: T.M. Robinson, *Heraclitus* (1987, University of Toronto Press).One note about my translation. In some cases, I've built on standard translations. For a few of my renderings, I've been a little more liberal in my translations. Heraclitus wrote in an oracular fashion, and in order to maintain this style, I have taken "poetic license" to ensure that the real sense of the epigram is apparent. The most difficult epigram to translate is the first one because it contains the concept *logos* (λόγος). Literally, this epigram translates as "All things happen according to the *logos*." What is the *logos*? Its most basic meaning is "word." Prior to Heraclitus, *logos* also meant "account," "language," and "story." During Heraclitus' times, *logos* could also mean "reason," "principle," and "explanation." Six centuries later in the Gospel according to St. John, it becomes *Logos* with a capital "L" and took on a theological meaning: "In the beginning was the Word." What is *logos* for Heraclitus? Some have identified it as "logic" or "formula." I believe that what Heraclitus means for *logos* is "the organizing principle by which the cosmos orders itself." This organizing principle manifests itself in the various patterns we recognize. Also, the *logos* is very deep, so it is able to manifest itself in many different ways. One final thought: Heraclitus, ever capable of being both literal and metaphorical at the same time, knew that the "word" is "spoken." And what does the cosmos speak? I believe that "patterns" is how the *logos* is spoken to us. Thus, my translation, "The cosmos speaks to us in patterns."

"The cosmos speaks to us in patterns."

1. γινομένων γὰρ πάντων κατὰ τὸν λόγον.

Find A Pattern. If the cosmos reveals its secrets to us in patterns, then we need to pay attention and listen for them. Indeed, we need to use all of our senses to discover new patterns. Fortunately, our minds are well-versed in this language. Much of what we call "human intelligence" is our ability to recognize and discover new patterns. We recognize similarities, cycles, arrangements, series, processes, flows, and behaviors. You find patterns by getting into a "pattern-seeking, pattern-finding" frame of mind. First you notice something. Then you focus your thinking and try to find something similar to it, occurring again or simultaneously. As poet Diane Ackerman put it: "Once is an instance. Twice may be a coincidence. But three or more times makes a pattern." Using this logic, have you noticed any "coincidental" things that fit into a larger pattern? **What patterns do you detect in your issue? What story do they tell?**

"A wonderful harmony arises from joining together the seemingly unconnected."

2. ἁρμονίη ἀφανὴς φανερῆς κρείττων.

Connect the Unconnected. Much of what we call thinking is our ability to connect ideas together. Why is "joining together the seemingly unconnected" so special? The more often the same ideas are brought together again and again, the more predictable they become, and the less thought they generate. Conversely, it is the connection of previously unconnected ideas that stimulates us to think, that make us say, "Aha!" and see our situation in a fresh way. Indeed, joining together apparently unrelated ideas lies at the heart of the creative process. It's the basis of invention, poetry, art, crime detection, humor, and problem solving. **What unrelated ideas can you combine?**

"Everything flows."

3. πάντα ῥεῖ.

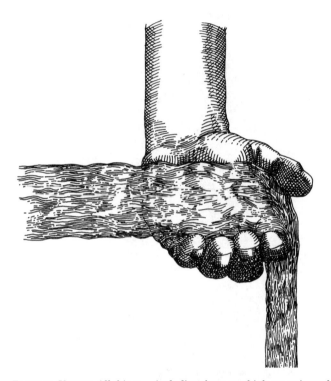

Focus on Change. All things — including those we think are quite stable — are continually changing, developing, and transforming over time. However, this "flowing change" is not taking place at an even, uniform rate. We can extend Heraclitus' water metaphor by noting that things "flow" at different rates. A glacier flows at one speed, a swollen stream at another, a lazy river at another, a flood at another, and a stagnant pond at another (it evaporates). So we also need to notice the rate at which the change is taking place. Indeed, if we don't see the changing forms, then perhaps we're not looking at things in quite the right way. For example, if you look at a block of iron over a two-minute period, you probably wouldn't say that it's flowing, but if you look at it over a two-year period, you begin to see rust, corrosion, and wear. And conversely, some things change so quickly that it's not always possible to see different things as being related. **What is the "flow" of your issue? Where will it be in the future? What patterns describe its behavior? Do you need to change your point of view to see the change?** ¶ **Appreciate the "Now."** If everything is changing, then we need to appreciate the "now" because soon it will be gone. If it's a bad situation, then take heart, because that too will be gone. **What is in the moment?**

"You can't step into the same river twice."

4. ποταμῷ γὰρ οὐκ
ἔστιν ἐμβῆναι δὶς τῷ αὐτῷ.

Update Your Assumptions. A flowing river constantly changes its contents and shape. It may look the same from moment to moment, but it never is the same. So it is with the cosmos: new things come into being, others die, and everything else changes. The world of yesterday is not quite the same as the world of today or the one of tomorrow. What worked yesterday may not work today, and what is improbable today could be tomorrow's "sure thing." Thus, it's important to continually update our assumptions about what is "real," and find solutions that are appropriate for the problems we encounter. Things may be similar to the way we've experienced them in the past, but they are never exactly the same. **What assumptions should you update? What is no longer true? What is now possible? If every situation is different, how can you improvise? ¶ You Are Changed.** By stepping into the river, you change both the river and yourself. Similarly, getting involved with a particular issue changes both it and you. **How is your dealing with this issue changing both it and you?**

"That which opposes produces a benefit."

5. τὸ ἀντίξουν συμφέρον.

Problems Force Us to Be Creative. Routines are the boon and bane of our existence. They're beneficial because they allow us to get things done without much thought. They're harmful because they can prevent us from developing a fresh perspective. The danger is that often we have integrated them so well into our thinking that we're no longer aware that we're being guided by them. Thus, we need an occasional jolt to wake us up and shake us out of our mental patterns. Here's an example: suppose you have a particular routine that allows you to reach a specific objective. Now, suppose one day there's an obstacle in your routine path — a problem if you will — that prevents you from reaching your objective. As a result, one of the following might happen: 1) you use your creative abilities to eliminate the obstacle; 2) you go around the obstacle and find another way to reach your objective; 3) in the course of the search, you find another objective that is preferable to the original one and that you wouldn't have discovered had you not been forced off the routine path; or, 4) you question whether you even need to reach your objective. Thus, opposition (in the form of confrontation, problems, obstacles, discontinuity) can provide a benefit. **What's creating opposition in your issue? Are there alternative ways to reach your objective? Is the objective you originally sought still desirable? What if your objective were unobtainable?**

"If all things turned to smoke, the nose would be the discriminating organ."

6. εἰ πάντα τὰ ὄντα καπνὸς
γένοιτο, ῥῖνες ἄν διαγνοῖεν.

Pay Attention to Different Types of Information. There is a great variety of information around us, but often we dwell on only a limited amount of it. Are you focusing on the right information? **What other senses can you use?** ¶ **Recognize Opportunities.** What if the concept you're working on were burnt to a crisp? Do you have the intuitive sense to sniff out an opportunity in its ashes and vapors? And if so, what would your next course of action be? To put this another way: how flexible are you? Suppose the world rewarded people who could write provocative poetry. Then one day the rules changed, and it decided to reward people who could do automotive repair work. And then still another day, it rewarded people who could grow food. How well do you adjust to changing circumstances? **If your concept were greatly transformed, what would the result be? What opportunities would be present?** ¶ **Ask "What If?"** Heraclitus has made a hypothetical statement and then followed it up with the consequences of such a hypothesis. This is the formula for asking "what if" questions and stretching your thinking. **What imaginative "what if" questions can you ask about your issue?**

"Lovers of wisdom must open their minds to very many things indeed."

7. χρὴ γὰρ εὖ μάλα πολλῶν
ἴστορας φιλοσόφους ἄνδρας εἶναι.

Be an Explorer. To create new ideas, you need the materials from which they're made: facts, concepts, knowledge, experiences, feelings, and whatever else you can find. You can look for these in the same old places. However, you're more likely to find something original if you become an explorer and venture off the beaten path. A good explorer has an "insight outlook" — that's the attitude that there's a lot of good information available, and all you have to do is find it. With an "insight outlook," you know that the different ideas you find have the potential to come together to form something new. If you go to an airport, you'll find ideas there. If you go to a museum, you'll find ideas there too. And the same applies to hardware stores, garbage dumps, circuses, political rallies, libraries, wilderness areas, restaurants, senior centers, sporting events, old magazines, and gardens. Indeed, the more divergent your sources, the more original the idea you create is likely to be. **How curious are you? Where else can you look for ideas and information? From what different areas can you borrow?**

"The most beautiful order is a heap of sweepings piled up at random."

8. σάρμα εἰκῆ κεχυμένον ὁ κάλλιστος ὁ κόσμος.

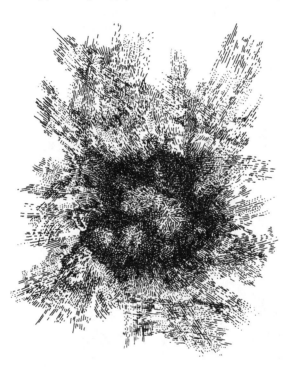

Find Meaning in Random Ideas. Take advantage of your mind's pattern recognition ability. If it can find meaning — in this case "beauty" — in something as humble as a "heap of random sweepings," then it can find it anywhere — even when none is intended. Look at the bark of a nearby tree. What shapes do you see? A map of Europe? Ocean waves? Your uncle's profile? Throw together stuff from different places — a Celtic signet design, vein distribution in a maple leaf, voter turnout percentages in Presidential elections — and you'll find some sort of pattern. Select something at random and relate it to your issue. For example: pick out the 10th word on page 204 of your dictionary. Look out your window and find the first thing that has "red" in it. Open a magazine and find the 8th full page ad from the front. What is its product? How do these relate to your issue? Open your mind up to things that have nothing to do with what you are currently doing. **Pick an object at random. How does it relate to your issue? What connections can you make? What patterns can you find? What similarities do you see? What light does it shed on your issue?**

"Those who approach life like a child playing a game, moving and pushing pieces, have the kingly power."

9. αἰὼν παῖς ἐστι παίζων,
πεσσεύων· παιδὸς ἡ βασιληίη.

Play With It. "Kingly power" means having mastery over a domain — be it a discipline, subject area, situation, or problem. This power comes from having an attitude ("those who approach life") similar to that of a child playing a game. This attitude allows you to play with the issue at hand, to "push and move" its various pieces and elements, to look at it in a variety of contexts, to experiment and try different things, and to find out what works and what doesn't. As a result of this play, you come to know and understand the different sides of the issue. From this the mastery arises. **In what ways can you "play with" the various pieces of your issue? How can you experiment? What new approaches can you try? What risks can you take?** ¶ **Laugh At It.** Humor is a wonderful form of play. Indeed, there is a close relationship between the "ha-ha" of humor and the "Aha!" of discovery. If you can laugh at a problem or situation, maybe you'll dislodge a few assumptions about the way you think about it, and perhaps come up with some fresh approaches. **What can you take less seriously? What humorous things can you say about your issue?**

"Knowing many things doesn't teach insight."

10. πολυμαθίη νόον οὐ διδάσκει.

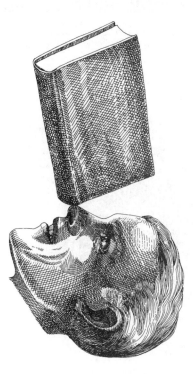

Play With What You Know. Knowledge is the stuff from which new ideas are made. Nonetheless, it alone won't make a person creative. The key to creative insight consists not so much in gaining new knowledge but in finding new ways of *thinking* about what you know. Creativity requires an attitude that allows you to play with and manipulate your knowledge so that it takes on new meanings. This is an attitude where you don't see each fact as a separate bit of knowledge but rather as a link in a chain of ideas. **What different ways can you think about what you know? In what different contexts can you put your issue? ¶ Use Your "Forgettery."** Knowledge is a great resource. In certain situations, however, ignorance can be just as valuable. Forgetting what you know — at the appropriate moment — can lead to good ideas. Without the ability to forget, the mind remains cluttered up with ready-made answers, and you never find the opportunity to ask the right questions. Remember: everyone has the ability to forget. The art is knowing when to use it. Indeed, novelist Henry Miller once said that his "forgettery" was just as important to his success as his memory. **What can you forget? What can you ignore?**

"Sea water is both pure and polluted: for fish it's drinkable and life-giving; for humans undrinkable and destructive."

11. θάλασσα ὕδωρ καθαρώτατον καὶ μιαρώτατον, ἰχθύσι μὲν πότιμον καὶ σωτήριον, ἀνθρώποις δὲ ἄποτον καὶ ὀλέθριον.

Shift Your Point of View. Context determines meaning. If you say "Make me one with everything" to a teacher of religious mysticism, it means one thing, but if you say the same thing to a hot dog vendor it means something quite different. Similarly, if an amusement park operator tells a middle-aged man, "I'll bring out the kid in you," one set of expectations will be created; but if an obstetrician says this to a woman in labor, a different result will occur. Much of creativity is the ability to take a thing or a concept and put it in different contexts so that it takes on new meanings. The first person to look at an oyster and think "food" had this ability. So did the first person to look at mold and think "antibiotics." As did the first person to look at the burdock burr and think "velcro fastener." And so do you if you have ever used a pen as "back scratcher," a potato as an "antenna," a box of marbles as a "musical instrument," or a clothes pin as a "toy." **In what other contexts can you place your concept? How would its meaning change?** ¶ **Think Best Case and Worst Case.** Heraclitus has described two environments: one "life-giving," the other "destructive." **What are the conditions that would allow you to be successful in your issue? What will cause failure?**

"On a circle, an end point can also be a starting point."

12. ξυνὸν γὰρ ἀρχὴ καὶ πέρας ἐπὶ κύκλου περιφερείας.

Reframe the Situation. Reality rarely presents itself to us with clearly defined boundaries. Rather, we impose our own order on the world through the concepts and categories of our language. If you change the concepts you use to describe a situation, you reframe it and change the way you think about it. For example: Is the beach the "end" of the ocean or the "beginning" of land? Is a twelve-year-old female an "old girl" or a "young woman"? Is the cocoon the "end" of the caterpillar or the "beginning" of the butterfly? Is water the "end" of ice or the "beginning" of vapor (or vice versa)? Is this the "last" sentence of all the sentences you have read up to this point, or the "first" one of all the ones you shall henceforth read? You could answer "yes" to any of these questions. It shows that a thing, idea, or issue can be framed in a variety of different ways depending on one's point of view. Using different words and concepts to reframe a situation is a vital creative thinking skill. It gives you flexibility in the way you approach the world. **How can you reframe your issue? What other categories could be used to define the situation?**

"Disease makes health sweet and good, hunger satiety, and weariness rest."

13. νοῦσος ὑγιείην ἐποίησεν ἡδὺ καί
ἀγαθόν, λιμὸς κόρον, κάματος ἀνάπαυσιν.

Look At the Other Side. Opposites define and complement one another. For example, it's very difficult to have a concept of "up" without one of "down," "hot" without one of "cold," "good" without "bad," "beauty" without "ugliness." If one ceased to exist then the other wouldn't have much meaning. Each puts the other in relief. Each is the "ground" from which the other stands out. Furthermore, we don't really appreciate or understand something until we have experienced or thought about its opposite. Thus, to better understand something, look at its opposite. Reversing your point of view is also a good technique for opening up your thinking. For example, suppose you are designing a solar cell. Posing the problem as an attempt to raise efficiency to 30% would lead your thinking in one direction, while asking how to reduce inefficiency to 70% would lead your thinking to a very different direction. Similarly, the shift in focus from "cure" to "prevention" in stating medical goals has changed the field of medicine. Remember, it's hard to see the good ideas behind you by looking twice as hard at what's in front of you. **How can you look at what you're doing in an opposite way?**

"The doctor inflicts pain to cure suffering."

14. οἱ ἰατροὶ τέμνοντες καιόντες.

Do the Opposite. Sometimes the best way to reach an objective is to use the reverse of the apparently "logical" approach. For example: 18th century physician Edward Jenner discovered the invaluable medical tool of "vaccination" by inoculating healthy people with a dangerous but usually non-lethal disease (cow pox) to prevent them from contracting a deadly one (small pox.) Try looking at what you're doing in a reverse manner. **How might employing a reverse strategy enable you to reach your objective?** ¶ **Cut.** If a part of a whole causes the whole to "suffer," then remove it. For example, a person editing a story might find a part that detracts or gets in the way of the whole and decide to cut it. This may "pain" the story's author but it is necessary to improve the overall work. **What in your issue needs to be pruned or removed? What unsatisfactory thing can you let go of? What pain will that cause?**

"The way up and the way down are one and the same."

15. ὁδὸς ἄνω κάτω μία καὶ ὡυτή.

Rethink Your Strategy. In Heraclitus' worldview, things are continually changing. Thus, every "way" or strategy that leads "up" (success, progress, fulfillment) can ultimately become the wrong one and lead to the "way down" (failure, missed opportunity, stagnation). Thus, we need to be flexible in what strategies we use and change approaches when necessary. For example, what works for the caterpillar doesn't work for the cocoon, and most assuredly won't work for the butterfly. Similarly, what's effective in parenting a two-year-old will be counter-productive when that child is a teenager. **Is the strategy that enabled you to get to where you are now the strategy you want to keep using? Conversely, is there an approach or strategy that you may have rejected early on that may be appropriate now?** ¶ **Try the Reverse Approach.** Heraclitus believed that unexpected things occur in the cosmos. Thus, if the "way down" and the "way up" are the same, then there are times when the "way down" (or reverse strategy) can lead to the destination of the "way up." Anyone who plays hard-to-get to be more attractive, gets away from a problem in order to solve it, goes to the city to be alone, or gives away one's possessions in order to feel rich is using this counter-intuitive strategy. **What reverse strategy can you apply?**

"A thing rests by changing."

16. μεταβάλλον ἀναπαύεται.

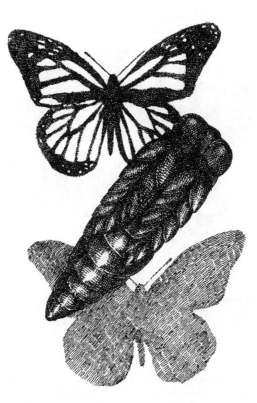

Move On. This paradox poses the counter-intuitive notion that change is more restful than staying in one place. It is resolved by understanding that in Heraclitus' worldview, everything is continually changing, and that it often takes less energy to move on to the next phase of a process than fighting to stay in the current one. It's like rowing a boat on a river: it takes more effort to remain stationary heading into the current than it does to go with the flow. **Where would your energy be better focused: on where you've been or on where you're going? Is it time for you to move on to the next phase?**

"Things love to conceal their true nature."

17. φύσις κρύπτεσθαι φιλεῖ.

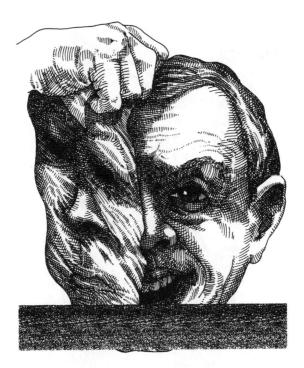

Look for the Hidden Order. Heraclitus believed that reality loves to conceal its true nature, that it is intentionally enigmatic. But he also believed that this enigma can be understood if we adopt a creative thinking mindset and look behind surface appearances to see hidden patterns. Heraclitus felt there is a reason for nature's disguise: truth is precious and we appreciate it more if we have to work to find it. **What truth aren't you seeing? What order is hiding in your concept? ¶ Look for Deception.** Deception plays an important part in life's workings. We see it in nature (animals camouflaging themselves for protection against predators; predators disguising their intentions in order to trap their prey), war (a military leader not showing his strength in order to lure an enemy into battle), sports (a team disguising one play as another to confuse the opponent), and politics (candidates hiding character flaws in order to get votes). **What is hidden from you in your issue? What would you like to be revealed? How can you conceal your real intentions? What benefits would that create for you? In what ways are you deceiving yourself?**

"Many do not grasp what is right in the palm of their hand."

18. ᾧ μάλιστα διηνεκῶς ὁμιλοῦσι τούτῳ διαφέρονται.

See the Obvious. Sometimes the most helpful ideas are right in front of us, but we fail to see them. Here's an example of people missing the obvious. If you study the evolution of the bicycle during the 1860's and 1870's, you will notice that both wheels start out at about the same size, but over time the front wheel gets larger and larger, and the rear wheel becomes significantly smaller. The reason was that initially the pedals were attached directly to the front wheel. Since there was no drive train on the bicycle, the only way to make the bike go faster was to make the front wheel bigger. The culmination of this trend was the "penny farthing" with a front wheel almost 1.5 meters in diameter. Needless to say, they weren't very safe. The curious thing about this whole development is that the solution for a better and safer bicycle was right in front of bicycle designers. The bicycles themselves were manufactured using drive train technology! Finally, someone looked up and made the obvious connection, and asked, "Why not use the drive train technology to power the rear wheel?" Within only a few years this safer model supplanted the penny farthing. **What resources are right in front of you? What are the most obvious things happening in your issue? What is so plentiful that you don't even notice it?**

"When there is no sun, we can see the evening stars."

19. εἰ μὴ ἥλιος ἦν, ἕνεκα τῶν ἄλλων ἄστρων εὐφρόνη ἂν ἦν.

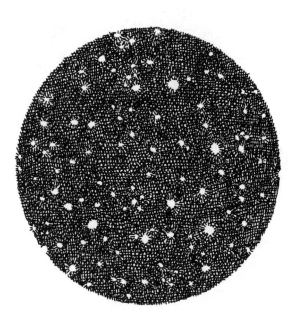

Suppress the Dominant Element. In this wonderful metaphor, the "sun" represents the dominant feature of a thing, situation, or relationship. Some examples: a person who dominates a group, a noise that drowns out the other sounds, a strong spice that overwhelms the other seasonings in a dish, a player who outshines his teammates, or an activity that squeezes out others. The "evening stars" represent either the less obvious aspects of a thing, or alternative ways of thinking about it. We don't see these because the "sun" (or dominant view) is so bright. When there is no sun (the dominant aspect is diminished), the stars (alternatives) are visible. To say this in another way: discovery often means the uncovering of something that was always there but was obscured by something more dominant. **What's the most dominant feature of your situation? How does your situation look when you ignore that dominant feature? What's changed? What new features come into view? What "stars" do you see? Similarly, what is the least important feature or function of your situation? What if that's all you noticed?**

"The barley-wine drink falls apart unless it is stirred."

20. ὁ κυκεὼν διίσταται μὴ κινούμενος.

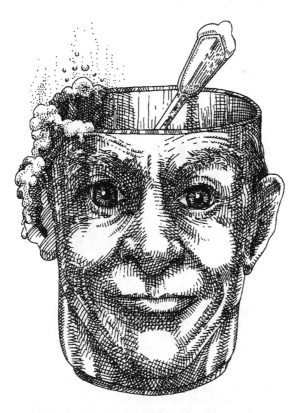

Stir Things Up. The barley-wine drink or "kukeon" was a sacred libation made by mixing together ground barley, grated cheese, and wine. If the whole were not continually stirred, the contents would stratify and the "kukeon" as such would cease to exist. Similarly, some things only achieve their being through the continuous interaction of their parts. **How can you stir things up in your issue?** ¶ **Mix Together the Right Conditions.** Some things only come into existence when the right conditions are present, for example: rainbows (when the sun is behind the observer, less than 42° above the horizon, and shining into rain), solar eclipses (when the sun, moon, and earth are aligned), or political revolutions (when there is economic downturn, vast social inequity, and an attractive new ideology). **What are the conditions for success? What pieces of your issue need to be stirred together in order for you to be successful?**

"Expect the unexpected, or you won't find it, because it doesn't leave a trail."

21. ἐὰν μὴ ἔλπηται ἀνέλπιστον, οὐκ ἐξευρήσει, ἀνεξερεύνητον ἐὸν καὶ ἄπορον.

Be Willing to Be Led Astray. Often what we're looking for leads to something much different. For example, physicist Karl Jansky improvised a new antenna to study the effects of telephone static. Instead, he discovered radio waves from the Milky Way galaxy, and in the process helped create the science of radio astronomy. Think of the times in your own life where one thing has led to something entirely different. (How did you get interested in your line of work? How did you meet your spouse? How about the times you've gone to the library in search of a particular book, and then found something even better on the shelf behind you?) As writer Franklin Adams put it, "I find that a great part of the information I have was acquired by looking up something and finding something else on the way." Expecting the unexpected is an attitude that consists of: 1) loosening your preconceptions about what you expect to find; 2) paying special attention to the anomalous and unusual rather than ignoring it; and, 3) using that as a stepping-stone to something very different. **What elements of your idea or problem can lead you in new directions? What would happen if you abandoned your original objective and followed the directions that open up? What unusual places might they lead to?**

"When we're awake, there is one ordered universe, but in sleep each of us turns away from this world to one of our own."

22. τοῖς ἐγρηγορόσιν ἕνα καὶ κοινὸν κόσμον εἶναι, τῶν δὲ κοιμωμένων ἕκαστον εἰς ἴδιον ἀποστρέφεσθαι.

Pay Attention to Your Dreams. Your dreams are symbols through which your unconscious mind speaks to you. Take advantage of them to help you resolve conflicts, inspire solutions, and suggest new approaches. How many times have you awakened from a dream and thought, "What was that all about? Why did I dream of catching bugs with my toothbrush? What did it mean that I appeared on stage with my son? Why were Sappho and Genghis Khan sewing a quilt on an airplane?" But if you think of the dream as a stimulant to your imagination, and interpret it in different ways, you may discover something that will lead your thinking in a new direction. For example, if you dream someone kidnaps your children, you might take it as a sign that you should spend more time with them. It might also mean that you believe that someone is stealing your ideas. Or perhaps it could mean that you're being too serious and therefore you should be more playful. Indeed, dreams may lead you to get an insight into a problem much in the same way one did for 19th-century inventor Elias Howe. His dream of being attacked by spears with holes through their points led him to change the design of his sewing machine needle (he put the eye near the point instead of its traditional position at the other end). **How can you relate a recent dream to a current problem?**

"Dogs bark at what they don't understand."

23. κύνες γὰρ καὶ βαΰζουσινμ ὧν ἂν μὴ γινώσκωσι.

Watch Out for Criticism. New ideas are different by nature. They can be threatening and disturbing to the existing order. Thus, most people have a warning device in their minds — a "barking dog" — to alert them to strange new ideas. Unless the new idea cleanly dovetails into what they are currently doing, a typical reaction will be: "It won't work," "I don't get it," or "It's dumb," rather than "Gee, what a great idea!" **What negative reaction do you expect? How can you quiet it? How persistent are you? How many times can you be told "no" and still push forward?** ¶ **Improve Your Concept.** If the "dogs are barking" at your idea, then there may be a good reason: perhaps the idea is not well thought out, not very attractive, not connected to anything, or — worst of all — you've done a lousy job of selling it. Your course of action should be to improve your idea. Consider the barking to be a compliment: at least you are getting someone's attention. If something isn't provocative or threatening, it's easier to ignore it than to bark at it. **How can you make your idea easier to understand? How can you make it more attractive?**

"Donkeys prefer garbage to gold."

24. ὄνους σύρματ᾽ ἂν ἑλέσθαι μᾶλλον ἢ χρυσόν.

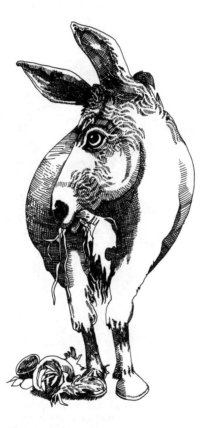

People Value Different Things. What is important to one person can be of little consequence to another. What is sacred to one group can be profane to another. What is unthinkable in one culture can be as natural as breathing in another. Thus, your "golden idea" may be just so much garbage in someone else's estimation— and vice versa. As the 18th century English wit Samuel Johnson put it: "So much are the modes of excellence settled by time and place that men may be boasting in one street of that which they would anxiously conceal in another." **Do other people value your issue the way you do? How do you need to educate them, i.e., help them understand your perspective? Do you need to educate yourself about their point of view?** ¶ **Significant Works Require Effort.** If you're lazy, you probably won't achieve or create something important. In Heraclitus' view, most people are too easily satisfied with the "easy garbage" than the more significant but "hard-to-get gold." **How willing are you to make your idea a success?**

"Every walking animal is driven to its purpose with a whack."

25. πᾶν γὰρ ἑρπετὸν πληγῇ νέμεται.

Failure Wakes Us Up. Like other walking animals, sometimes humans need a good "whack" to get them focused on their purpose. One thing that "whacks" our thinking is failure — it jolts us out of our routines and forces us to look for fresh approaches. To a great extent we function according to the principle of negative feedback. When things go smoothly, we don't think about them. Often it is only when things fail to do their job that they get our attention and we realize that the current approach is not working, and that we need to come up with some new ideas. **How would failing affect what you're currently doing? What would you feel free to try?** ¶ **Disrupt Success.** Is success good? Sometimes the answer isn't so obvious. Just as failure can lead to something good, sometimes success can lead to something bad: it can lock us in one way of doing something so that we get the attitude, "If it's working, why change it?" This attitude prevents us from trying new approaches that may lead to something better. To be innovative, sometimes we have to oppose or destroy current ways of viewing things. Remember: every act of creation is first of all an act of destruction. **What previously successful assumptions can you challenge? What can you try that has a lesser chance of success?**

"There is a greater need to extinguish arrogance than a blazing fire."

26. ὕβριν χρὴ σβεννύναι μᾶλλον ἢ πυρκαϊήν.

You Are Not God. Self-confidence is essential to your success as a creative human being. That's because when you create new things, you expose yourself to failure, frustration, ridicule, criticism, and rejection. A sense of your own worth fuels you to persevere to make your idea a reality. There is, however, a line between a healthy sense of one's abilities and something more grandiose. If you are repeatedly successful, there is the temptation to believe that you have found the "success formula," and are no longer subject to human fallibility. With an arrogant attitude, you cease paying attention to differing points of view and divergent information. You screen out the "boos" and amplify the "hurrahs." You believe that you're not subject to the same constraints as others. This is devastating to the creative process; in a world that is continually changing, every "right" idea or strategy eventually becomes the "wrong" one. The ancient Greek concept for arrogance is "hubris," and it was seen as a precursor to one's downfall; anyone proud enough to challenge the gods will be burned by the gods — as surely as night follows day, destruction follows arrogance. **Where is ego adversely affecting your judgment? Where have you been successful in the past when dealing with similar issues? Has success made you less receptive to other approaches?**

"I searched into myself."

27. ἐδιζησάμην ἐμεωυτόν.

Look to Yourself. Each of our lives is unique. We each have our own dominant senses, our own metaphors, our own memories, our own idiosyncrasies, our own successes and failures, accomplishments and disappointments. Draw upon your wealth of knowledge and experience. **What insights from your life can you use? What from your own history is similar to your current issue?** ¶ **Trust Your Intuition.** Heraclitus believed that consulting one's intuition was an appropriate method for gaining insight into a situation. Our subconscious mind is constantly assimilating information from the outside world. At some point, it turns this information into answers — hunches — that have relevance to the issues we deal with. **What hunches have you had lately? How can you apply them to your issue?** ¶ **Express It In Your Own Terms.** Sometimes problems are presented to us in a format in which we feel little flexibility. A good creative rule of thumb is: "Never state a problem to yourself in the same way as it was brought to you." **How can you redefine the issue so that it more clearly reflects your own terms?**

"Your character is your destiny."

28. ἦθος ἀνθρώπῳ δαίμων.

You Set Your Direction. Life doesn't happen to us in a random, haphazard way. Rather, we constantly determine our own course through the decisions we make: what to pay attention to and what to ignore, what time to get up and when to go to bed, how hard to work and how much to play, how much to enjoy the moment, how much to save for tomorrow, what to share with others and what to keep private, when to persist and when to relent. Heraclitus says that our character is the "program" that determines what kinds of choices we will make in various situations. Character consists of the parts of your basic nature that you let manifest themselves (and by corollary also those you suppress). It is shaped by one's upbringing, education, culture, and experience. Do you tend toward being hard-working or lazy? Impetuous or cautious? Humorous or serious? Compassionate or tough-minded? By-the-book or likely to improvise? Verbal or visual? Skeptical or gullible? Aggressive or passive? Selfish or altruistic? Intuitive or detail-oriented? Introverted or extroverted? **What parts of your character are likely to help you succeed in your issue? What parts may interfere?**

"The Sun will not deviate from its routine, because the avenging Furies, ministers of Justice, would find out."

29. ῞Ηλιος γὰρ οὐχ ὑπερβήσεται μέτρα· εἰ δὲ μή, ᾿Ερινύες μιν Δίκης ἐπίκουροι ἐξευρήσουσιν.

Identify What Cannot Be Changed. For the cosmos to be "ordered," there are some things that need to be consistent and predictable. The sun is one of these: it must rise in the east, set in the west, travel close to the horizon in winter, and be nearer the meridian in summer. If it behaved unpredictably, e.g., rose in the west or remained stationary in the sky for hours at a time, there would be chaos. So it is with many other things in our world: if they deviated from their routine, order would be lost. **What are the unalterable parts of your issue? What provides the basic order?** ¶ **Consider the Consequences of Change.** Sometimes when we alter something, forces are set in motion that can wreak havoc to the status quo and cause horrific results. Heraclitus uses the mytho-religious metaphor of the "avenging Furies of Justice" for the fierce reaction that change can bring. It is also the fear of these forces of reaction that prevents change. **What Furies (reacting forces) hold you in check? Are the Furies real? What havoc would be wreaked if you changed a supposedly unalterable part of your issue?**

"The sun is new each day."

30. ὁ ἥλιος νέος ἐφ᾽ ἡμέρῃ ἐστίν.

Imagine Different Futures. Our world is constantly changing: new laws and rules are enacted and others are no longer enforced; new social and political movements gain momentum while others become spent and irrelevant; new technologies gain ascendance pushing aside the increasingly obsolete ones. Each of these situations — and any other where change is involved — provides a new environment in which some things will thrive and others will be diminished. **What changes in future conditions would be beneficial for you? What would be disastrous? What can you plant today that will grow in a substantially different environment tomorrow?** ¶ **Improvise.** If the sun is new each day, why limit yourself to approaches and solutions that you've used in the past. **Where can you improvise?** ¶ **Give It Another Try.** If things are different, then it's possible that what didn't work yesterday has a chance of working today. **What can you try again that didn't work in the past?** ¶ **Forgive and Forget.** If the sun is different today, why not forgive the animosities and disagreements from yesterday? Perhaps the storms and clouds have given way to something brighter today. **What can you forgive in your issue? On what issues can you begin with a clean slate?**

About the Author
(The First Right Answer.)

Roger von Oech is the founder and president of Creative Think, a Menlo Park, California-based consulting company specializing in stimulating creativity through seminars, consulting, and products. His presentations and publications have stimulated the creativity of many millions of people around the world.

Prior to starting Creative Think in 1977, he was employed by IBM.

Dr. von Oech is a Phi Beta Kappa graduate from Ohio State where he received both the President's Scholarship Award and the Scholar-Athlete Award. He earned his Ph.D. from Stanford University in a self-conceived interdisciplinary program in the "History of Ideas."

He is married to Wendy, and they are the parents of two children, Athena and Alex.

About the Author
(The Second Right Answer.)

Sometimes I think the mind is like a compost pile. It contains a variety of ingredients stewing together toward the end of producing something useful. Some ingredients aid the process, some hinder it, and others are inert.

Many of the ideas in my own compost heap have come from my work as a creativity consultant in industry. I picked up the other ingredients from a variety of experiences. My sixth grade teacher, Mr. Rodefer, taught me that being creative and being obnoxious are sometimes very similar, but that they are not the same thing. He taught me how to differentiate the two by giving me a creative license. We had an agreement: I'd run a lap around the school yard for every obnoxious act, and he would reward me for my new ideas. I learned to take chances. In addition to running 128 laps that year, I did some very creative things.

I learned about competition from swimming. I remember my sixteenth summer when Paul McCormick and I spent successive weeks beating each other's time in the 100 free. The competition made us both faster.

Some of my ideas came about hitchhiking around the country — I put over 30,000 miles on my right thumb in a five year period. I remember one ride in particular in which I learned about supply and demand. The driver was a Montana cowboy who was bootlegging pornography from San Francisco to Utah. He had discovered that there were people in the hinterlands who would pay three times the cover price for his four-color commodity.

I wrote my doctoral dissertation on the twentieth century German philosopher Ernst Cassirer, the last man to know everything. From him, I learned that it's good to be a generalist, and that looking at the Big Picture helps to keep you flexible.

In having my own business, I've discovered that you can have the greatest idea in the world, but if you can't sell it to other people, you're not going to get very far.

As the father of two children, I've had it reinforced that we're all born with the ability to be creative and look at the world in different ways.

And in doing my own work, I've learned that people enjoy having their minds stimulated, and that a whack on the side of the head can be a positive experience.

I hope you enjoyed this book. If you have any comments, thoughts, or creative experiences you'd like to share, I'd be delighted to hear from you.

Address all correspondence to me at:

Creative Think
Box 7354
Menlo Park,
California
94026
USA

e-mail: roger@creativethink.com

Happy Whacking!

R.v.O.